mental space

I CAN CLEARLY

SEE
NOW

mental space

how to find clarity in a complex life

Tina Konstant and
Morris Taylor

www.yourmomentum.com
the stuff that drives you

What is momentum?

Momentum is a completely new publishing philosophy, in print and online, dedicated to giving you more of the information, inspiration and drive to enhance who you are, what you do, and how you do it.

Fusing the changing forces of work, life and technology, momentum will give you the right stuff for a brighter future and set you on the way to being all you can be.

Who needs momentum?

Momentum is for people who want to make things happen in their careers and their lives, who want to work at something they enjoy and that's worthy of their talents and their time.

Momentum people have values and principles, and question who they are, what they do, and who for. Wherever they work, they want to feel proud of what they do. And they are hungry for information, stimulation, ideas and answers …

Momentum online

Visit www.yourmomentum.com to be part of the talent community. Here you'll find a full listing of current and future books, an archive of articles by momentum authors, sample chapters and self-assessment tools. While you're there, post your work/life questions to our momentum coaches and sign up to receive free newsletters with even more stuff to drive you.

If you need more drive for your life, try one of these other momentum titles:

soultrader
personal career strategies for life
Carmel McConnell

reinvent yourself
tactics for work, life and happiness - yours
J. Jonathan Gabay

be your own career consultant
how to unlock your career potential and help yourself to your future
Gary Pyke and Stuart Neath

managing brand me
how to build your personal brand
Thomas Gad and Anette Rosencreutz

coach yourself
make real change in your life
Anthony M. Grant and Jane Greene

change activist
make big things happen fast
Carmel McConnell

lead yourself
be where others will follow
Mick Cope

happy mondays
putting the pleasure back into work
Richard Reeves

innervation
redesign yourself for a smarter future
Guy Browning

the big difference
life works when you choose it
Nicola Phillips

hey you!
pitch to win in an ideas economy
Will Murray

snap, crackle or stop
change your career and create your own destiny
Barbara Quinn

float you
how to capitalize on your talent
Carmel McConnell and Mick Cope

from here to e
equip yourself for a career in the wired economy
Lisa Khoo

grow your personal capital
what you know, who you know and how you use it
Hilarie Owen

PEARSON EDUCATION LIMITED

Head Office:
Edinburgh Gate
Harlow CM20 2JE
Tel: +44 (0)1279 623623
Fax: +44 (0)1279 431059

London Office:
128 Long Acre
London WC2E 9AN
Tel: +44 (0)20 7447 2000
Fax: +44 (0)20 7240 5771
Website: www.business-minds.com

First published in Great Britain in 2002

© Pearson Education Limited 2002

The right of Tina Konstant and Morris Taylor to
be identified as Authors of this work has been
asserted by them in accordance with the
Copyright, Designs and Patents Act 1988.

ISBN 1843 04016 6

British Library Cataloguing in Publication Data
A CIP catalogue record for this book can be
obtained from the British Library.

10 9 8 7 6 5 4 3 2 1

Cover and concept design by Heat.
Production design by Claire Brodmann Book
Designs, Lichfield, Staffs.
Typeset by Northern Phototypesetting Co. Ltd,
Bolton
Printed and bound in Great Britain by
Henry Ling Ltd, Dorchester

The Publishers' policy is to use paper
manufactured from sustainable forests.

Dedication…

We were able to complete this book and dedicate it to the memory of Robert Taylor and the futures of Keetah and 'Mo' Konstant mainly due to Edith Taylor (Auntie Molly) and Alan and Simon. Their house in Aberdour – Spens Cottage – gave us space, time and amazing views over the River Forth.

Aberdour 2001

contents

chapter one
getting into mental space

mental space

In its simplest terms, mental space is *thinking space* and *time*; the *moment* you take between an event and your reaction that gives you time to respond in the best way.

Circumstances or events around you are merely that: *events.* How you respond, feel or think is dictated by your interpretation of these events. You can *choose* to react in a positive or negative way to what goes on around you. The aim of this book is to help you *create thinking space in your mind* so that you can *respond* to the world in a way that will benefit you instead of *reacting* in ways that might be inappropriate and do you more harm than good.

The main difference between us is how we *think*

How we perceive and interpret the world is unique to each of us. In a very stressful situation, one person might panic and 'fall apart' and another may become calm and focused. The difference between the two reactions starts in the mind of the individual.

Since we are unique, there is no universal recipe for a 'good life', three steps to perfect living or five steps to absolute happiness. We have greater needs and desires than can be fulfilled in seven easy steps to a great future. We're more complicated and interesting than that.

For any one 'recipe' to work, all human beings would have to respond identically to life situations. We don't. Imagine if ten people were being treated for a headache and all were given the same treatment. The treatment might work for five of them. That same treatment could cause a more severe headache in another two. It might have no effect on two more of the patients, and it could cure something unrelated in the last one. No one solution can possibly suit everyone. We are all too different.

Instead of giving you definitive steps to success and happiness, this book will show you how you can use your own mental space to have more choice in your response to your world in such a way that you achieve what you want, *your* way.

This book is *not*:

◆ Step-by-step instructions on how to live your life.

◆ A series of things to do that will make all your worries disappear on the spot.

◆ A promise that you will immediately live your dream because all your desires will materialize if you visualize hard enough and use the right affirmations.

◆ A series of exercises you have to practise every day.

◆ Lecture, conjecture and theory.

◆ A hidden message that will be revealed to you 'when you are ready'.

This book *is*:

◆ Practical, applicable and straightforward.

◆ A series of strategies that you can incorporate into your daily life without taking all your time and energy.

◆ A collection of tools and ideas to pick and choose from as and when required.

◆ A challenge to you to live differently by thinking, feeling and reacting differently.

◆ Ways to put the passion back in and improve your quality of living by easing the pressure of your life.

This book is especially for you if you:

◆ Don't feel in control of your life.

◆ Would like more time to really enjoy what you have but feel overstretched.

◆ Want straightforward solutions that will have great impact on you life.

◆ Have an underlying good feeling about your job and your life, know that you can be, do and have more, but perhaps think you don't have the time or energy to make the necessary changes, and as a result, feel overwhelmed, stressed and dissatisfied.

This book may also help you if you happen to be thoroughly or partly fed up with just about everything and would like a different way of approaching life.

Reading this book for best results

It is not necessary to read this book from beginning to end. To get the best out of *Mental Space* familiarize yourself with the contents, determine what you want from the book at the moment, read that only, then return to the book later when you need more information on a different subject.

The following speed-reading strategy will help you get the most out of this (and any other book) in the shortest possible time:

◆ Read the *five-step system* for effective reading.

◆ Read this chapter; it contains an *outline* of the book.

◆ Use the *five-step system* on the book.

The five-step system for effective reading

The five-step system will help get you through huge quantities of material quickly. It is straightforward, it works *simply because you use it*, and it requires *no* practice.

In the true spirit of creating mental space, this strategy is an excellent system for reading *any* non-fiction material. Use it to clear your in-tray at work, your mail, that pile of unread magazines, newspapers, and any non-fiction book, research or learning material.

Step One – Prepare
First, ask yourself two questions: What do you already know about this subject? What questions do you have? Then, determine exactly what you want from this book. What is your purpose? Why are you reading it?

Step Two – Preview
Familiarize yourself with the *structure* of the book. Go through the book quickly; look at paragraphs, chapter outlines, cartoons, graphics, and general layout.

Step Three – Passive reading
Your familiarity with the language used in any book is a major factor in determining the speed at which you will be able to read. Take a minute to clarify your purpose, and then skim over the pages at about *one page per second*. Think about your purpose and skim the text. Look for words that stand out. If your purpose is to find the answer to a specific question, look for words that will alert you to the answer. Don't spend more than one second per page. Highlight pages that you will want to return to.

Step Four – Active reading
This is the first time you will begin to *read* the book. First, read the introductions and the summary sections. Then, read the first paragraph of each section and the first sentence of each paragraph (and the last sentence if the paragraph is long). No more! The temptation at this point will be to get back to reading the book from

front to back. Again, highlight the sections and pages you will want to return to (it's OK to write in a book if it's yours – it's not like a school text that will be used by others).

Step 5 – Selective reading
Read only what you need or want to read.

To help you decide exactly what you might want from this book this time around, each chapter is outlined with references of where in the book you will find exercises that relate to each topic.

A brief outline of the contents of mental space

One of the most important chapters in this book is **Chapter 2**. Regardless of how well you plan or manage events, without *focus and concentration*, you will achieve little. It is important to highlight at the beginning that daydreaming can take as much focus and concentration, and indeed energy, as action. *Active daydreaming* is key to generating and using mental space. The intention is to help you to think and to do what you set out to do instead of allowing your mind to wander and drift.

In **Chapter 3:** your whole body is a thinking organ. A gut feeling is more than just a sensation. Learn how to read and trust your body's reactions to life.

In **Chapter 4:** learn how to use your greatest asset and largest sense, your imagination.

If you're going somewhere, you need to know where you are (in time and space), where you've been and where you want to go. **Chapter 5** will take you through a thorough inventory of your life that will give you a solid foundation on which to build new dreams, ideas and realities. The purpose behind these strategies is to allow you to build your future without destroying your present or changing your past. The methods in this chapter will help you prevent *vision overload*: wanting something but not knowing how to get it, and living in a dream instead of turning your dreams into reality. You will also learn how to break habits and change damaging behaviour.

Chapter 6 is more than handling accounts; it is about developing an abundant and healthy attitude towards money. The main reason people develop money problems is because they were never taught how to make it, use it or spend it. This chapter will provide strategies that will lay the foundation for continued financial education.

Chapter 7 discusses *time*. It is not 'time management'. You cannot manage time. *Tempus fugit* regardless of what you do or how you try to manage it. This chapter will, instead, help you to manage events. How to manage what you want to do in the time you have to do it in and how to choose and prioritize events and experiences.

Chapter 8 discusses your *perception on the world and how to handle perceived chaos.* This chapter can also help you get your life in perspective, identify *real* issues and problems, and, most importantly, how to consider the consequences of your actions. Learn how to work out the facts instead of acting on your interpretation of the facts, appreciate a little chaos, love surprises, identify the difference between a surprise and a crisis, and enjoy this totally unpredictable planet and everyone in it. This chapter will also shed light on the effects of physical clutter in your life and how to preserve your mental space when the world around you is in chaos, despite your best efforts.

Whereas Chapter 8 discusses your perception of the *world,* **Chapter 9** considers your *self-concept.* Your perception of yourself: your level of confidence, self-image, self-appreciation and self-esteem, takes place in your head. Fill your head with the right stuff about you. When you do what you want to be doing with your life, many things that you previously held to be true about yourself will change. This chapter will encourage you to give yourself space to be your best, even in difficult circumstances.

In discussing *conflict and how to handle it,* **Chapter 10** contains ways to get difficult people out of your face and out of your head and how to create mental space by putting distance between you and conflict. Instead of reacting without thought and often inappropriately, you will have space and time to think and act carefully, rationally and calmly, diluting the situation instead of exacerbating it. The strategies in this chapter help you keep your head clear and get out of conflicting environments unscathed. You will also learn that having mental space in a conflict situation gives you space to listen – the lack of which more than likely caused the conflict in the first place.

Chapter 11 gives strategies to help your long- and short-term memory. Three main reasons for apparent memory 'failure' are disorganization, distraction and a lack of awareness of your surroundings. The more organized you are and your thinking is, the more mental space you will have, allowing yourself to *be present.* Being present is the key to improving all areas of memory.

Chapter 12: no matter how much you don't go looking, even during the most ordinary day vast amounts of information will somehow seek you out. Organized information-management skills help prevent you from becoming overwhelmed. The five-step reading system described earlier is a proven method. Knowing how to gather information is one thing; distilling it and putting it to good use is another.

Being *inside* the ball, or perhaps worse, *being* the ball, does not allow you to play the game. **Chapter 13** contains techniques used by some of the greatest thinkers in history. Einstein said that ideas do not appear in a vacuum, and solutions don't always 'just happen'. They are usually a result of an active imagination. This chapter contains strategies to help you find your own solutions and be more creative under pressure.

Chapter 14 is intended to help those suffering from excessive *perfectionism.* Being perfect is fine as long as you don't use perfectionism as an excuse not to start or finish what you set out to do. Key questions are: Who sets your standards? Do you set standards for others and fail to meet them yourself? Are you time perfect (on time but short on quality) or quality perfect (great on quality but never on time)?

The world is full of people, we need each other, and we need to tolerate and be tolerated by others. **Chapter 15** is about *relationships* – personal, social or business. Identify relationship problems *before* they become an issue. Resolve problems quickly and avoid cross-contaminating problems between different environments (home and work, for example). Also, learn how 'taking your problem to lunch' can be useful.

Chapter 16 for further development, contains websites, books and other sources of information to help you continue to learn and clear your space.

Navigating Mental Space

For the most part, each chapter is self-contained. The following menu cross-references related ideas and strategies.

Chapter	Other chapters to refer to for information on this subject
2, 3 and 4	These three chapters contain the basics for developing mental space. Read them in conjunction with any other chapter in the book.
5: Mental space: past, present and future	Chapter 6: Mental space makes money Chapter 7: Creating time with mental space Chapter 15: Relationships and mental space
6: Mental space makes money	Chapter 5: Mental space: past, present and future
7: Creating time with mental space	Chapter 5: Mental space: past, present and future Chapter 8: Perception: the world around you
8: Perception: the world around you	Chapter 9: Self-concept Chapter 10: Mental space, aggression and conflict Chapter 15: Relationships: and mental space
9: Self-concept	Chapter 5: Mental space: past, present and future Chapter 8: Perception: the world around you Chapter 10: Mental space, aggression and conflict Chapter 14: Perfect (and when good is good enough) Chapter 15: Relationships and mental space There is, in fact, something in every chapter in the book that will contribute to developing your self-concept.
10: Mental space, aggression and conflict	Chapter 8: Perception: the world around you Chapter 9: Self-concept Chapter 14: Perfect: (and when good is good enough) Chapter 15: Relationships and mental space

chapter two
focus, concentration and attention

mental space

momentum

Do you ever daydream … gaze through the classroom window … contemplate the wall as your computer screen flickers at the edge of your awareness … drift somewhere pleasant as someone talks to you?

Your eyes glaze … you stare into space, absorbed in your thoughts, your feelings, plots, characters, a book you are reading, something you intend to do tomorrow, or wish you had done today, that conversation you had yesterday … last month … last year …

Your attention shifts … other aspects of the same thing … something unrelated … another time … another place … you're gazing into a different space … near or far … up or down … left or right … sensations are arising and changing … tingles … pressures … softnesses … sequential … simultaneous … shifting … eyes … heavy … light … flutter … wide … then someone interrupts … something entirely unrelated … irrelevant, out of place. You return to the here and now, perhaps gently, perhaps with the tiniest of jolts.

Daydreaming shows that you can focus. You can concentrate.

Perhaps not about what an employer or teacher has asked you to work on. Whatever absorbs you to the exclusion of everything else will be important to you in one way or another: positive or negative, joyful or sad, fleeting or long term …

Without concentration there is no mental space.

It's easy to allow your head to fill with mental chewing gum or wandering, fluffy, random chaos.

To many people, concentration does not come easily for two reasons:

◆ We can be distracted very easily.

◆ There can be much to distract us.

Concentration is focused attention

Attention has certain properties:

◆ It is **dynamic**. Try focusing on one thing only and notice how long it is before your mind wanders. The aim of meditation is to enable you to focus on one thing without losing attention and it's very hard for most of us.

◆ It is **undivided.** Try listening to more than one conversation at the same time. You will probably hear bits of each but it is unlikely you will absorb either fully.

◆ It follows **interest**. Boredom extinguishes attention.

◆ It is maintained by a series of **discoveries**: new ideas and insights.

There are several kinds of attention:

Voluntary attention is when you are totally absorbed by what you are doing and distracted by nothing. When you voluntarily pay attention to something, you do so naturally. You don't have to force yourself to concentrate, you find yourself *absorbed*.

Autopilot often happens when you are carrying out routine tasks. When driving, for instance, you may arrive at your destination and be unable to immediately recall the journey.

Dispersed attention is caused by too many activities going on simultaneously, or by lack of interest. A sense where everything attracts your attention and you can't focus on anything for longer than a few moments.

The aim of this chapter is to help improve your ability to control

mental space

momentum

your voluntary attention so that you are able to focus your attention willingly and fully, even in situations where you would otherwise find it difficult to concentrate.

When divided attention works and when it doesn't

Attention is linear. If you are already carrying out a sensory task using one or more of your sensory channels (vision, hearing, touch, taste, smell) and you then begin doing something that requires a high level of attention, you will have to make a choice consciously or subconsciously. For instance, if you are driving in dangerous conditions you will notice that your attention is total. If the radio is on you will probably ignore it. If, on the other hand, the road is clear and the conditions are good, you might be able to drive, listen to the radio and have a conversation at the same time. The instant a dog runs into the road, your attention will focus entirely on driving. The change occurs in milliseconds.

Interest and motivation

The more interested you are in what you are doing, the easier it is to concentrate.

Remember when you were last so engrossed in what you were doing that you lost awareness of time? Nothing else distracted your attention. You were totally interested and motivated towards a goal. There are two words to take particular note of – *motivated* and *goal*.

When you know what you want to have happen (a *goal*), and the specific reasons you want it (*motivated*), then the desire (*interest*) to complete the task successfully helps you concentrate more fully.

If, however, the job is boring and it is hard to find either motivation or interest, then deliberate action is required:

- Carry out one of the breathing exercises outlined in Chapter 8. Take a little time to still yourself and gather your thoughts.

- Write down your reasons for doing the task, how long you estimate it will take you to finish, the most challenging thing about the task, the easiest part of the job, and what you are going to do when the job is finished.

- If your mind drifts, *speak out loud* as you write down your plan. Your attention will focus very quickly, your desire to complete the task will take over, and your concentration will improve.

Time out

The stress response prevents concentration and inhibits thinking.

If you feel out of control, anxious, tired for no reason, irritable or agitated, sit back for a moment and do nothing. Just breathe and relax. Yes, even if you are overworked and overwhelmed. It's worth it.

- Try to establish the situation or circumstances you are responding to.

- Take stock of what needs to be done:

    - to resolve the situation;

    - to complete the job in hand.

- Be aware of the time available to you.

- Decide the actions you have to take.

- Prepare.

- Act.

Worrying about how you will do the things you have to do is a distraction in itself and achieves little.

Distractions and solutions

The two main ways in which concentration can be interrupted are *internal* distractions and *external* distractions.

In an ideal world we would do only what interests us … in the right environment, when we had as much time as we needed, when we wanted to. Life, however, is not always like that. We often have to things in which we have no particular interest, at a time and place not suited to us and, all too often, with a deadline.

Distractions are not just the things that happen *around* you. Your internal state can be just as distracting as a constantly ringing telephone, perhaps more so. Have you ever tried to focus your mind with a thumping headache? Distractions interfere with both thinking and action. The more you can reduce them, the more chance you will have of successfully completing what you set out to do in the time available to you.

In this chapter, we will explore a range of distractions and ways of working around them.

Maintaining concentration

Take breaks often – To ensure peak concentration, take 5-minute breaks every 30 minutes if you are focused on a specific (intense) task. If you are doing a number of different tasks, you could stretch your work time to between 70 and 90 minutes before you take a 5-20 minute break. Pay occasional attention to your body as you work. When you start yawning, drifting into non-relevant daydreams, making mistakes, re-reading passages, or developing a headache, it is time for a break. If you work through the symptoms of tiredness, your concentration and your ability to think and understand what you are doing will diminish rapidly, as will the quality of work you produce. Taking a break does not mean lying down and going to sleep for 20 minutes (although it is an idea to do that occasionally) – go for a walk, have some protein if you are thinking, have some carbohydrates if you are doing something physical, drink a lot of water, do something different.

Purpose – Know your reasons for doing what you are doing. The clearer your purpose, the easier it will be to concentrate, even if you would prefer not to. If you have *no* reason, you will probably give up fairly quickly.

Think actively – Take notes, write down ideas, speak to people, especially if you are feeling tired or if the job is challenging. The more senses you use, the more alert you are likely to remain. Imagine eating a meal and all you could do was look at it. You couldn't smell it, taste it, feel the texture of the food or hear the sounds of cutting and slicing a juicy dish. All you could do was see it and eat it. How much would you enjoy that meal? The enjoyment *is* the sensory appreciation of the meal: the taste, smell, texture and presentation of the food. Otherwise, it's just 'fuel'. The same applies to thinking. We are taught from an early age to think only with our minds. When you build mind-maps, take notes, discuss and *actively* think, concentration becomes more like the meal that you can see, taste, smell, hear and feel. You almost always remember a meal when the company is good and the surroundings are pleasant. Treat concentration and thinking like a good meal; you will *amaze* yourself.

Time – Set a definite time limit on each task. Break tasks into chunks. The chunks should be small enough to be easily manageable, yet big enough so that you feel that you are steadily moving toward achieving your goal. Be realistic. As you work, if you find the chunks are too big or too small, stop and reassess. Be flexible.

Coping with external noise

Unless you can concentrate while there is background noise, you will want to minimize the noise around you. There will always be some external noise over which you have little control. If you work in an open-plan office, you might find the noise distracting. There are several things you can do to minimize external noise and distraction.

Earplugs – These can be effective and, if you get the right type, comfortable. Most good chemists and specialist safety shops will supply them. Try a few different makes and types.

mental space

Music – Wear earphones with appropriate music. Music without words and not too loud. For maximum concentration, Baroque music is best, with approximately 55–60 beats per minute. Make sure it's not melancholy and only play music you enjoy. Mozart, Vivaldi and some of Beethoven's works are good for concentration. Experiment with music. Put one composer on for 20 minutes, change to another and then compare how you feel or how well you concentrated.

Define your space – If your desk is in an open-plan office, create a visual barrier between you and the rest of the office. You do not have to build a wall. All you need to do is put something on your desk that reaches eye level. This will provide a psychological barrier between you and the distracting environment and make it easier to cope with.

Working around others – If you work in a noisy environment and have a task that requires high concentration, arrange your time so that you do the task while others are out of the office – at meetings or during lunch. Don't miss lunch or work too late too often. Just rearrange your time so that you are in the office when others are out. This may be more manageable if your company operates flexitime.

Coping with internal noise

Mental noise happens when your mind wanders. If you haven't made a firm decision to complete a task in a given time, the internal talk in your head might sound like this: 'I don't have the time for this … X really needs to be done now … Y will have to move to this afternoon … I should be doing Z …' You will be unlikely to be able to focus on *anything* long enough to complete the original task and you will be wasting time.

Make the decision – Choose to allocate a certain amount of time to the job. After the decision is made, most internal talk will disappear. You can then focus.

Physical distractions

Tiredness – When you are tired it is almost impossible to concentrate. If you are physically tired, take a break and go for a short nap. If you are mentally tired, but not physically in need of a sleep, take a walk in the park. If you are unable to do that, several other strategies are open to you:

◆ Cut the time you spend concentrating down to 10–15-minute chunks.

◆ Drink plenty of water.

◆ Do aerobic exercises during your breaks – jump up and down and get the oxygen flowing.

◆ Every few minutes breathe deeply and stretch.

◆ If you play music, make it suit your purpose: up-beat for energy, slower for relaxation.

◆ If you work through your tiredness, make sure you have a very, very good reason.

◆ When you are finished, stop and take a well-earned rest. Tiredness is often a sign of a job well done; rest is a reward.

◆ Avoid working through the night or excessively long hours.

◆ Avoid sugar, salt and wheat.

◆ Avoid caffeine. For maximum performance, you want to be alert, not jittery.

Stress – If you are stressed, it is better to stop for a short time even if you think you don't have the time. Stop, breathe, relax and evaluate the job. Drink some water and carry on. Being stressed does not make you work any faster or effectively. Think: 'Can I do this another time? What is stressing me and how can I reduce that?' Talk to somebody about it and see if that helps or brings up new ideas for resolution.

mental space

momentum

Hunger and thirst – Hunger is a serious distraction. Similarly, if you eat too much, concentration will be impaired. If you have a large amount of work to do, avoid eating too much at once and avoid excess sugar and starch. Another cause for poor concentration is dehydration. Your body is mostly water. Most people don't appreciate just how much water they need to replenish what is lost through natural hydration. By the time you feel thirsty, you are already dehydrated. If you are getting a lot of physical exercise or if you are in a hot country, you may need as much as six or eight litres per day. If you are sitting at a desk, three to four litres should be enough. Drink plenty of water even if you don't feel like you need any. Avoid tea and coffee, because the caffeine in them will dehydrate you more than a lack of water will.

Environmental distractions

Stuffiness – Ensure you get plenty of *fresh* air. If you can't get it in the office, get it during breaks. Be as comfortable as possible without feeling sleepy.

Light – Daylight is best. If there is none, then there should not be too much contrast between the levels of light under which you are working and the rest of the room. This helps prevent eyestrain. The main source of light should come over the shoulder opposite to your writing hand.

Desk and chair – Make sure your desk and chair are the right height. When you sit on the chair you should be able to sit back in the chair supporting your back with your feet flat on the floor. If you cannot reach the floor, place a block at your feet or use a proprietary footrest that puts your feet at the right height and angle. Your desk should be large enough to take everything you need for the work in hand.

Work distractions

Plan your day – If you don't know precisely what you want to achieve, distractions come easily. At the start of your day, write down everything you want to achieve. Include in the list enough time for quality recovery time (QRT) both during and after a task. Once you plan for it and use it, you will notice that taking time to relax will help rather than hinder you through the day.

Set ground rules – After you have started something, don't let anything distract you from completing it without a very good reason. Have you ever started mowing the lawn or doing the dishes only to get distracted onto something else, then don't really want to go back to it? When you start something, *finish it*. This will not only improve the quality of your work; it will increase the amount that you can achieve. You will also experience a relaxed satisfaction once the job has been done.

People distractions

Few people have the luxury of being able to work without interruption. There is always someone somewhere demanding attention.

If you can, estimate the time that you will need for a job and put up a 'do not disturb' notice. If you are unable to do that, deal with interruptions like phone calls and people wanting to see you by consciously breaking off from your task and paying attention to the interruption, or have a disciplined call-back system that your contacts can come to rely on.

If the phone rings or someone approaches you while you are concentrating:

- Finish your current thought.

- Mark the place where you stopped, and write a few words to remind yourself what you were thinking.

- Quickly revise in your mind or on paper your understanding of what you are doing.

- Then give attention to the interruption.

When the interruption is over and you can return to your task, to minimize lost changeover time:

◆ Take a moment to recall your understanding of the task.

◆ Recall and re-affirm your purpose.

◆ Decide the time for a manageable chunk.

◆ Get to it.

Music and mental space

Sounds that surround you can make or break a working environment. Have you ever been in an office and felt a silence so uncomfortable that you must whisper even though you know you shouldn't have to? On the other hand, some workspaces are so full of music and noise that within moments you feel you have to leave? A song might come on the radio and you either have to switch it off or have the urge to turn it full blast, open the windows and sing along.

Music is a powerful phenomenon, so much so that certain chords and sounds were banned by the rulers of China because they knew music affected people.

Some music is so depressive and negatively motivating that it has been banned by the BBC (see *The Secret Power of Music* by David Tame; for details, see the resource section in Chapter 16).

For our purposes we will look only at the music that will help your levels of concentration.

The important thing about music is that it is appropriate to your current purpose and that you enjoy and appreciate it. If, while trying to concentrate, you listen to music that you don't like, you will become agitated or stressed.

The music you select for consideration should have certain properties:

- Relatively gentle, but not to the extent that it induces sleep.

- No words.

- Low and unobtrusive volume.

- Variety.

Here are some suggestions:

- Bach – Largo from Harpsichord Concerto in F Minor.

- Corelli – Largo from Concerto Number 7 in D Minor, Opus 5.

- Vivaldi – Largo from Concerto in D Major for Guitar and Strings.

Some people assert that loud and intrusive music helps them concentrate. So, it is entirely up to individual taste.

Brain food – eating for maximum concentration

Every cell and molecule in your body changes and develops depending on what you put into your body.

The air you breathe, the liquid you drink, and perhaps most importantly the food you eat all affect your body.

If you need to concentrate for an extended period, the ideal eating pattern is *little and often* – of the right stuff. In our fast-food society, we tend to eat on the run. High-sugar and high-fat foods reduce your energy levels.

Top ten tips on focus, concentration and attention

1 Have a purpose.

2 Relax.

3 Do one thing at a time.

4 Take plenty of breaks.

5 Think with more than your mind. Write down ideas. Explore ideas. Create new thoughts.

6 Be excited by your thinking.

7 Allow time for creativity and imagination to happen as your mind wanders and daydreams.

8 Talk to others, and test your ideas.

9 Never assume that someone staring into space is doing nothing – for them, silence may facilitate their most active and creative thinking.

10 If you mind insists on wandering, take a good break and get back to your task later.

Final thought

A delegate on one of my workshops said that when he had something to do that took focus and concentrated attention, he would go into a cleaning cupboard in his office. He would jam the door shut and stay there until he was done. The cupboard became known as 'Jim's thinking room'. His colleagues began to use the space when they needed to think. The reason this space was so good is that only one person could fit inside.

chapter three
mind your body

Like a radar system, your body is constantly picking up information from your environment. When something requires attention (impending danger, for instance), your body gives you a combination of physical and emotional messages. These messages may be feelings or 'little voices'. Have you ever had a feeling that you were being stared at or that you were being followed? You are constantly receiving messages from your body. They are sometimes ignored.

The more in touch you are with your body and you learn to understand and trust your instincts, the more likely you are to understand the information your body is trying to give you and make better decisions in difficult situations.

This chapter contains information that will help you:

◆ Be more sensitive to your instincts and take them into account when making decisions.

◆ Reduce internal conflict and panic in challenging situations.

◆ Help you respond more calmly to your environment.

◆ Reduce stress.

◆ Increase health and wellbeing.

You should only have to practise these techniques for a little while before they begin to benefit you. Some strategies will suit you, others may not. Try each of them to find those you prefer.

Listening to your heart

When my yoga teacher taught me the following heart focus exercise, he told me that it was derived from Tonglen, a Tibetan meditative breathing practice. It can help you recognize stress responses and quickly transform them as they arise. He said that if I practised it at least five times a day for at least a month, my automatic response to events that previously stressed me would become much calmer.

Initially, it took about two to three minutes to experience calm. After a few days, I was able to become calm in seconds. The more I practised, the easier it was to respond appropriately to everyday events that bothered me from time to time. I used it often to become calm during stressful business meetings without others being aware. Before tackling challenging topics, I worked on simple things first. You can get a friend to help you with this.

Identify – *ten seconds*

◆ Think of something that you might ordinarily respond to negatively.

◆ Take a little time to become aware of your thoughts about it.

◆ Allow your thoughts to give rise to associated feelings or emotions.

Imagine and shift – *30 seconds*

◆ If you have a picture in your imagination, try to settle any movement in it.

◆ Play with the picture.

◆ Make it smaller in your mind.

◆ Move it away or step back from it.

◆ Now become aware of your heart centre (the area of your chest immediately surrounding your heart).

Activate and breathe – *20 seconds*

◆ As you remain aware of your heart space, notice your breathing.

◆ Pretend that you could breathe *through* your heart.

◆ Take a little time to try.

◆ Continue pretending that you are breathing through your heart.

◆ Recall a time when you felt appreciated and you knew the appreciation was *sincere*.

◆ Focus on the *feeling* that you had at that time.

Ask – *30 seconds*

◆ Continue to focus on that feeling of appreciation.

◆ Pretend that you are able to have a conversation with your heart.

◆ Ask your heart to think about the topic.

◆ Allow your heart a little time to answer.

◆ Pay attention to any intuitions or sensations that arise in you.

◆ Gently become fully aware of your surroundings here and now.

What did you notice?

When you do a reality check on your answers, how do they compare with what you thought previously?

After I had been practising this for several years, I attended a weekend workshop run by the Institute of Heart Math. They have a similar technique, and they have experimental evidence. You can visit them on **www.hearthmath.org**.

Body watching

The purpose here is to increase your awareness of your whole body: cells, muscles and blood flow. It is extremely relaxing and helps get rid of aches and pains:

◆ Choose a place were you feel safe and secure and where you won't be disturbed.

◆ Sit or lie down and make yourself comfortable.

◆ Imagine you can see inside your body, either from the inside or from the outside (experiment to find out which you prefer at different times).

◆ Go through your body, starting from the surface, and work your way into the centre of your body. Imagine being inside your skin. What does the layer between your skin and muscle look, feel or sound like? Explore the skin all over your body from your toes to your scalp. Then go deeper and explore your muscle fibre. What colour are your muscles? What is the texture? What is attached to your muscle? How fast or slowly are your muscles moving? Is there a space between your muscles, or are they packed tightly together? Next, explore your blood vessels. What colour is your blood? Is it really only red, or are there other colours in there too? Are the walls of your veins and arteries smooth or rough? Once you have explored every inch of vein or vessel, explore your bones. Are they hard all over, or are there tender, soft areas? Are they moist or dry? What joins them? What flows inside them? How are they attached to your muscles? Finally, explore your organs? Are they working quickly or slowly? What is going in and coming out of them? Are they comfortable or not? What kind of energy flow is there in your body? Is there enough water? Look at every part of your body.

◆ After you have explored your whole body, ask if there is anything you can do to make it healthier.

◆ Listen to the response, then act on it.

mental space

momentum

If you do this regularly, you may notice that small aches and pains disappear. Also, if something really is wrong, you will have a better chance of noticing it sooner because you will be in touch with your body and general health condition.

Surround awareness

This demonstration needs two people. The implications of it go beyond simply being aware of what is going on around you. Have you ever gone to an interview or met someone new and noticed that you move around in your chair until you are comfortable? Or how someone can be standing next to you and you feel uncomfortable for no obvious reason, yet as soon as they (or you) move, even just a little, the discomfort eases?

Most people are sensitive in one way or another to some of their immediate space.

Some people don't like anyone standing behind them; others don't notice it at all. My personal discomfort happens if I am standing in front of someone's desk when they are sitting behind it. It feels like I'm getting my homework marked by a teacher who is being too liberal with a red pen. If you are aware of where you are most or least comfortable in your personal space, you will be able to position yourself (say at a meeting or interview) so that you feel safe and comfortable. If you are with someone who looks uncomfortable, be aware that you might be sitting in one of his or her sensitive spaces.

Try this:

◆ Sit in a chair or stool in the middle of a room.

◆ Have someone you trust stand about two metres in front of you.

◆ Eyes open or closed, ask your partner to walk around you slowly in a circle.

◆ Notice the sensations in your body and any changes in your breathing. If you begin to feel uncomfortable, ask your partner to stop moving, notice their location, then ask them to move on, each time noticing where they are standing when you feel most or least comfortable.

◆ After you have done it once, experiment with distances and the combinations of you and your partner sitting and standing, eyes open, eyes closed. Ask the person you are working with to walk a circle around you about one metre in diameter, and again at three or four metres in diameter.

◆ Notice any differences when you try this with someone you don't know quite so well.

A good extension to this experiment is to check your surroundings in public places. Next time you are out having lunch or coffee, close your eyes and mentally imagine walking around your body, noticing where you feel any discomfort. Then, open your eyes and look around the room. What objects or people are in the places in the room where you felt uncomfortable?

Managing pain

Pain is information. It is also one of the greatest distractions.

Have you ever tried to work when you have a headache, backache or stomach cramp? When you are in physical pain or discomfort, all thinking stops.

In addition to being useful for some chronic and acute pain, the following technique can be useful for headaches, in particular migraine. It can also help with hangovers, and will usually stop hiccups within seconds.

However, symptom manipulation procedures must never be used to mask symptoms that have not been assessed by a medical or dental practitioner. If you have any recurring, chronic or unexplained acute symptoms, you must consult your doctor or dentist and allow them the opportunity to assess whether further investigation is required. For example, musculoskeletal pains may require physiotherapeutic, orthopaedic, chiropractic or other investigations/interventions.

If your medical practitioner has prescribed painkillers such as anti-inflammatory drugs to manage your symptoms, it is important to discuss this process with your doctor. Ensure he or she is happy with what you are doing and that no other factors need be accounted for. It can be dangerous to change the dosage of some drugs without the guidance of a medical practitioner. This is especially true, for example, with steroids. It is crucially important to check with your doctor.

Alleviating pain

If you can, scale your symptoms from one to ten – where ten is the worst. Raise a finger or an arm and allow yourself to become sensitive to that finger or arm as you watch it. The process outlined below may help alleviate some physical or emotional symptoms:

◆ Hold your arm out/finger up as if it were an indicator – like a temperature gauge on a car that can tell you how strongly you are experiencing those feeling. On a scale of one to ten (ten being the worst), how bad are your symptoms?

◆ As you continue watching your arm/finger, allow it to become so sensitive that it goes up if the feelings get worse and down when you feel better. Your arm/finger might vibrate or tremble a little; that's fine.

◆ Continue to focus on your arm/finger for a moment, and even if there is no observable movement or affect, notice what number you are experiencing now.

◆ Continue to focus on your arm/finger until you notice the pain diminish to zero.

Please remember the medical precautions. All pain is information. Notice it, find the cause, and consider changing your behaviour in a way that will prevent the pain from reccurring.

Top ten tips on minding your body

1 Be as healthy as you can. The more you take responsibility for your body, the less interference you will get from aches and pains.

2 Pain is information, so pay attention to it.

3 Trust your instincts: they are often right.

4 Spend at least a few moments each day reading your body.

5 Relax!

6 Trust the instincts of others.

7 Get plenty of quality sleep and exercise.

8 Be aware of your surroundings and the effects of the location of yourself and others.

9 Slow down. Your body sometimes takes time to deliver the message.

10. When making decisions, ask your body first.

Final thought

What if your elusive unconscious is not in some part of your brain that will never be fully understood or tapped, but is your entire body? Every cell, molecule, thread or fibre, feeling, sensation, instinct or ache, message or movement, physical, chemical, emotional, electrical or magnetic activity? In fact, the workings of your unconscious mind. If you knew how, you could read it like a book.

chapter four
mind's eye

One main difference between how Einstein thought and how most other people think is that his method was more disciplined. Take a minute to think about what goes through your mind in a typical day. What are the chances of generating a theory of relativity based on what presently occupies your mind? Give yourself a mark from one to ten (one = no chance, ten = I would have but Einstein just happened to get there first).

Great thinkers treat thoughts as *things*. Nikola Tesla pioneered the telephone repeater, rotating magnetic field principle, wireless communication, radio, fluorescent lights, and more than 700 other patents. He built, tested, modified and let them all run in his imagination. Then, still in his mind, he fixed what went wrong, then he built the real-world version.

Einstein said that he thought almost entirely in images, shapes and pictures; that mathematical formulas and theories came after the creative, explorative thinking – perhaps as a way of demonstrating and proving them to others.

Using your imagination constructively gives your mind the stuff it needs to be *productive* (create new ideas) as distinct from *re-productive* (create more of the old).

One reason why you might find it difficult to discipline and focus your thinking is because although it is fairly easy to start, shortly after you start to think, your mind wanders. Try this experiment: silently, say the alphabet backwards and in between each letter say the corresponding number: Z, 26, Y, 25, X, 24, and so on. Did you notice the letter at which your mind drifted off to something else?

One way to prevent drifting is to think out loud. Try the Z/26 to A/1 exercise again. This time, speak out loud. Unless you *consciously* stopped it, you probably got to the end quite easily. The emphasis is on *conscious*. When we think silently in our minds, it is easy for us to drift into a daydream. No harm in that. Most people spend at least some of their day daydreaming. The frustration comes when you want *specific focus* and can't do it.

Brain states

Most people function at the beta level of consciousness. Beta frequencies are about 14 cycles per second. The most productive states for creative thinking are the alpha (7–14 Hz) and theta (3–4 Hz) states. To understand the relevance of these cycles, human behaviours correspond to certain frequencies: anger (11 Hz), aversion (4.5 Hz), suicide (6.66 Hz), paranoia (4.5 Hz) or depression (6.66 Hz) *Remote Viewing*, Tim Rifat). When you understand how your mind works on a biological/mechanical level, it may be easier to consciously bring yourself out of a depression or negative mindset towards more positive and productive behaviours by manipulating your brain states. The following exercises may help.

The alpha and theta states are the optimum states for learning quickly and thinking creatively.

When you are in a positive mindset and in alpha or theta, you are physically relaxed, breathing deeply, eyes either closed or defocused, your attention inwards. These states, although good for learning, are also the preparation for sleep. This exercise will help make your thinking constructive (i.e. awake and purposeful).

Active daydreaming

Either do this exercise with a friend who can take notes of what you say during the exercise, or use a tape recorder.

- Write a single sentence summarizing what you are working on or thinking about, whether it is just one question or an entire subject, a theory, an idea or a problem.

- As well as being powerful, your mind is habituated. If it has a habit of wandering, it may not appreciate being focused. Set a timer for 10 minutes (if you are just beginning) and 45 minutes. If you are 'in the flow', you don't have to stop when the timer rings. If you don't set a time, after doing the exercise for only a few minutes you might think you have been at it for ages and stop before you really get going.

- Next, sit back, close your eyes, inhale and exhale deeply a few times, and give yourself permission to relax.

- Pose your question to your mind and then start to describe, *out loud*, all the images that come into your head. Just talk. It doesn't matter what the images are, what you imagine or think you imagine; don't disregard anything. Just speak. It is important to speak out loud for two reasons: you won't miss anything and you are more likely to stay awake.

- When the alarm sounds, you can stop or choose to continue until you feel you have had enough or you have come across an answer, idea or piece of inspiration that you sense might warrant further investigation.

- Take a short break then listen to the tape or study your friend's notes. Then, organize or categorize your thoughts.

- If working with a friend, swap over. You can both choose to compare notes afterwards.

Effective mental discipline

Imagine that you had to tell someone about the subject you are learning or a problem you are working on. Before you can explain an idea to someone in a way that *they* understand, you have to understand and integrate it yourself.

Einstein believed that even though the final *product* of invention was tied to a logical structure, the *invention* itself was not a product of logical thought.

Active daydreaming allows your mind the apparent paradox of disciplined freedom to create new ideas and concepts. The final stage is organizing the seemingly illogical stream of images and thoughts into a logical structure that you will be able to develop or perhaps explore further at some later date.

Visual thinking

We are all born as natural learners. Babies and young children absorb enormous amounts of information: entire languages, social skills, sensorimotor co-ordination ... As we grow up, and as the natural unconscious process of learning becomes conscious, whenever we learn something new, we are more aware (sometimes painfully so) of most of the pieces of information we absorb as we try to make sense of and understand the subject.

It's not learning that's difficult: it's our perception or approach to new information.

Our imagination works almost entirely in pictures. When you think of your front door you don't think the words 'front door', you *imagine* your front door. Yet when we are learning, we tend to think in words instead of pictures. Take a moment to be aware of how you are reading right now. Is there a voice in your head speaking the words to you as you read? Is a picture forming in your head or are you 'seeing' nothing at all, just 'hearing' the voice? Most people read and learn by relying only on the sound in their heads as they 'speak' to themselves. Consider the contradiction. Your mind naturally thinks, imagines and dreams in pictures, yet when we learn, read and try to make sense of new information, we use words, which are linear and hardly adequate to describe fully what we 'see'. Einstein believed that the spoken word had little to do with thinking. His notebooks consist almost entirely of drawings, maps and diagrams illustrating his thinking.

Applying visual thinking

Thinking in pictures, especially if the subject you are working on is abstract, is not always easy unless you are used to it. There are several ways to develop your ability to convert what you read into pictures as you learn. Why should you want to do this? Do you remember a novel better than you remember the contents of a textbook? Take a novel and a textbook on a topic in which you have no interest, neither of which you have read. Read a few paragraphs from each, then take a moment to consider what went on in your head. While you were reading the novel, you might have heard the words in your head as you read, and, if it was well written, you probably also saw pictures. The story may have unfolded in your head like a film. While reading the textbook, you might have heard the words, but did you see any pictures? This time, select a textbook on a subject in which you *are* interested. Compare what happens when you read that with what happened when you read the one you were not so interested in. Just like the novel, the most interesting textbook is more likely to generate images in your head. It is easier to remember a story or something we are interested in because as we read, learn and think about it, we think in pictures – the language of the brain.

Some people might not see pictures easily. These exercises can help develop your ability to visualize.

Using your hands to see

This needs two people. It might seem a bit touchy–feely, but that's because it is – in the literal sense.

Use a blindfold to inhibit vision. The blindfolded person will be presented with a variety of stimuli: touch, sound, taste or smell. The purpose is to encourage the blindfolded person to describe what they hear, smell, taste or feel by describing the *pictures* they see in their heads when they are presented with the stimulus. If you put their hand on a warm radiator, for instance, they cannot say, 'It's warm'. Encourage them to describe what warm might look like if they turned it into a picture. If they cannot find a picture immediately, start on the edges: ask them to describe what colour it might be, then what shape, then any movement. Gradually, from the images, a picture of the feeling will emerge.

The key here is *safety* and *permission*. As soon as someone puts a blindfold on, they trust you. Don't present them with *anything* alive (even if it's a family pet) or anything that might harm or startle them (for example, anything too hot or too cold). The more relaxed the blindfolded person is, the easier it will be to generate visual images. And remember, it'll be your turn next!

Developing imaginative perspective and visual thinking

Allow yourself to be comfortable. Look at your surroundings. Then, close your eyes and describe your surroundings out loud, in as much detail as you can. Notice whether it is easier to recall and describe shapes, colours or textures. Focus on the attributes of each object; describe the shape, size, colour, texture and any movement it makes. Next, consider each object in the room from another perspective. Take a little time to imagine what the back of the object might look like: the part you can't see. Describe all of your surroundings in terms of what you *cannot* see. Now, change your perspective again: imagine what these same surroundings might look like if you were as small as an ant: a plant stem might become a tree trunk, for instance. Finally, take an imaginative leap: imagine you *are* the object; describe the room (including the person sitting in the middle of it) as if you were that object. Give it life, imagine what a day in the life of a light bulb might be like, and describe it from that perspective in as much detail as you can. Other than being fun, this exercise will help develop your imagination as well as your ability to turn words into pictures and pictures into words. To increase the entertainment factor, do this exercise with other people. And remember – do it out loud.

Top ten tips to develop your mind's eye

1 Remember: visualization is simply the use of imagination, and *everyone* has an imagination.

2 Practise active daydreaming. The more you do it, the more constructive it will become.

3 Relax and give yourself time to come up with clear pictures.

4 Practise imaginative perspective by exploring everyday objects, from every angle, in your mind.

5 Keep a notebook next to your bed in which to write down your dreams. This will help develop your ability to retain and interpret images in your mind.

6 When you meet people, look at them carefully and with full attention. When you are no longer with them, re-create their face and surroundings as clearly as you can in your mind.

7 When you find your mind repeating past events and drifting mundanely, observe your thinking, determine the importance and relevance of it, and change your thinking to something more interesting.

8 Don't bore yourself with stupid thoughts. If there is no one else around to entertain you, entertain yourself.

9 Ask 'what if?' questions.

10 Have fun with your thinking and visual imagination. You have no idea what you are capable of until you think about it.

Final thought

We are born brilliant; it just takes time to realize it. Some of the greatest thinkers in history did their best work late in life. Don't think that because you are that 'certain age' you have passed your peak. You are the only one responsible for what goes on in your head and what comes out of it.

mental space

momentum

chapter five
mental space: past, present and future

Getting what you want from life would, on the surface, seem to be straightforward – decide what you want, then do it. There is no trick. However, the frustrating thing is that once you have decided what you want your future to be, your past and present keep interfering.

Your vision might, for example, be to get a great job, to go sailing every weekend, to retire at 45, or lots of travel. It's easy to make that decision. It takes a split second to decide what you want. *Getting it* is more complicated because your present, past and future are continuous. They don't just go away when you decide you want your future to be different.

Who you are, where you are, where you have been, and how you got where you are today are not going to change. Your perception of it may. That's where mental space comes in.

To achieve your new future, you have to disengage from your past behaviours, habits and responses and change your attitude towards present weaknesses, complications and frustrations. Consider the answer to the question. 'For X to become true, what else will have to become true?' To create a new future, what has to change for it to become true?

Sorting out the past and present in preparation for a great future

Most people leave the complications of their lives unsorted until they die. It is their will that others sort it out for them. Your life will be richer and more fulfilled if you take the time to organize it *now*.

This chapter takes you through a sequence intended to help you *evaluate* your present, *sort out* your past and *clarify* your future. A straightforward and practical method of determining what is important to you, what you want to do with your life, and what has to become true for it to happen. This might only take an hour or so, but the actions you decide upon might take months and years. This is the start; the rest is up to you.

Present inventory

If you are going somewhere, it helps to know where you are starting from.

This first step will help you build an inventory of your present life. Take time to do this. Since it is *your* life you are sorting out, first time round do it by yourself. Repeat it later with family, friends or anyone else influenced directly by your decisions. The most important thing to remember is that *you are responsible for yourself* first. If you make all of your choices based on what you think other people need or expect from you, you will never be the best you can. Nor will you be the best you can for anyone else.

Copy this page (or download it from **www.yourmomentum.com**) then complete the table.

Area in life	Percentage of time spent each month	Quality (poor or good)	Change required (yes or no)
Health Work/career			
Health, fitness and personal care			
Hobbies/personal interests			
Family			
Social life			
Holiday time			
Spiritual development			
Quiet time alone			
Education/further development			
Financial awareness and control			
Home maintenance and upkeep			
Eating			
Sleeping			
New pursuits and adventures			
Reading			
Keeping up to date with world affairs			

When you have included every aspect of your life on this list (what you presently do and what you *wish* you were doing), and you have determined how much of your time is spent in each area, take the time to decide what is best and worst in your life.

There are usually just a few obstacles in our lives that get in the way of everything else.

If, for instance, you feel that you are not earning enough, you might be in the wrong job. If you moved to something that paid better, your problems may disappear. Or you might need to learn how to organize and manage your money.

Once you have evaluated your present situation, look at each part of your life. What really needs to change? Your present relationship? Your job? Your location? You? Troubles in your life are rarely due to someone else.

The magic of choice

If you currently have financial problems, and if you think you have no choice but to carry on working each day, week and month to earn more money to pay interest on debts that increase each month because you are living on credit, take a moment to imagine you had a choice. Just pretend. Some of your choices might be:

◆ Learn how to fully understand your financial situation and how money really works.

◆ Change jobs and increase your salary.

◆ Change your lifestyle to fit your income rather than overspending each month.

◆ Learn how best to invest what money you do have.

◆ Educate yourself further and develop your skills.

◆ Get your whole family to pull together (i.e. tell them the real position you are in) and adjust the way you live.

◆ Ask for help from professionals. Get a good bank manager and enlist their help.

Instead of excuses, make choices. That may need courage , and it will take time, help, support and encouragement. If at all possible, don't do this by yourself. Get people you trust to rally around you.

Emotional inventory

Now that you have taken account of your present financial status, take time to account for your present emotional and rational self. When change has to happen, it has to start in your thinking. Do this next task with no holds barred. No one needs know what you include, although it might help to do this with someone who really knows you and who you trust.

Complete this table (also available on **www.yourmomentum.com**) truthfully and fully. Do it several times, at different times of day and in different moods. Your responses will very likely be quite different depending on how you feel at the time.

Area in life	What you like about yourself in this role	What you don't like about yourself in this role	What you would ike to be true about yourself in this role, and what you have to do to make it happen
Work/career			
Health, fitness and personal care			
Hobbies/personal interests			
Family			
Social life			
Holiday time			
Spiritual development			
Quiet time alone			
Education/further development			
Financial awareness and control			
Home maintenance and upkeep			
Diet and eating routine			
Sleeping			
New pursuits and adventures			
Reading			
Keeping up to date with world affairs			

Be honest with yourself when you consider these questions. What do you like about yourself? What do you not like about yourself? What are your strengths and weaknesses? What aspects of your emotional life prevent you from being your best and living the life you choose? What is it about *you* that gets in your way?

The next question is what is it about other people that gets in your way?

Social inventory

Not everyone is good for you or has your own best interests at heart. Friends and even family often prefer it if you have problems and weaknesses because it means that you will not stray very far or change very much.

One reason that people don't make big changes in their lives is fear.

You may worry that if you change, your friends, colleagues or family won't know, love or understand you any more. This social pressure is immense. We learn to live with it when we are very young and vulnerable. One of our earliest lessons is that if we don't do what people want us to do, they will be angry with us and push us away. Our need for recognition and appreciation is immense. From a very young age, we learn that social acceptance is important if we want social support. The price we pay for this support can sometimes outweigh the acceptance we get from society.

Those who really care about *you* (rather than their own needs) would be horrified if they thought that you were limiting your own happiness and success through a fear of causing them discomfort. Not making choices for yourself because you are concerned about other people is not a valid reason to inhibit your personal development.

The people you surround yourself with as you build your new future should be people that you trust and love. Even they might need some talking round if the changes you want to make are radical or drastic. Do it right, and you will *all* be happier for it. People who distract you from your vision, sap your energy, criticize and undermine you are often trying to make *themselves* feel better. Identifying those who are good for you and those who are not is vital.

This might hurt. Tact will be necessary. But it will be worth it.

◆ Make a list of everyone you know and connect with at any level. Include friends, family, colleagues and professional services.

◆ Describe your relationship with them.

◆ On a scale of one to ten, note how you feel about seeing each person: one being you dread it, ten being you look forward to it immensely. If you avoid someone at every occasion, that person is a one; if you look forward to seeing them on every occasion, that person is a ten.

◆ How do you feel about yourself when you are with each person? Do you feel good about yourself, happy, strong and confident, or do you feel a bit nervous, inferior, or apologetic for being you?

◆ How safe do you feel around each person? Could you divulge your deepest secret and they would still think good of you, or do you feel insecure and unsafe around them?

◆ Finally, consider each person and determine whether the relationship you have with him or her is as it is because of something you are doing right or wrong, or something *they* are doing right or wrong. If your relationship with someone is bad because of the way you are treating them, then you can choose to change. If the relationship is difficult or unstable because of how they are treating you, then you can choose to distance yourself safely or confront them. Whatever action you do take, please make sure that it is carefully thought out, considerate and appropriate.

Take a good look at the people in your life and make decisions about them. They are to be respected and treated in the best possible way. But you don't have to love or be loved by everyone. Make your choices. Give the people in your life your best and you will get the best from them.

Your past

Your present is a result of your past decisions. Your future is determined by the decisions you make now.

It is impossible to live in the present if you continuously live in the past.

You have choices: embrace it, ignore it or let it go.

Imagine this:

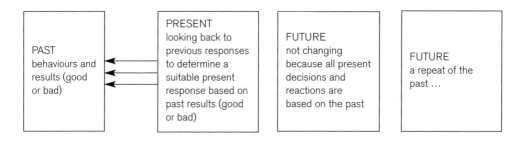

Do you know anyone who whenever an argument or disagreement arises, relives his or her past grievances, choosing to focus on years of being the victim of wrong-doing, even though it might be entirely unrelated to the present specific issue?

If you relate everything in the present to the past, it becomes very difficult to move forward. You will have no new ideas. No new dreams.

The past in comparison to the present and the future is inadequate. It will never live up to what we want it to be.

How often have you re-enacted a disagreement in your mind? Mentally, you got the opportunity to say what you should have said. But in reality, you never will. It's over. The only way you will ever get to say what you wanted to say is to re-create the disagreement at some time in the future and then, having rehearsed your lines, try to say what you meant to say the first time. Trouble is, the other party in the argument is unlikely to co-operate entirely, so it won't be perfect. In doing that, all you are doing is reliving your past and not moving forward.

Living in the past prevents you from creating new patterns and living a better life.

What is past is past. Learn from it and let it go. If you continue to judge yourself and others, you will never have the courage to be better because of your fear of repeating old inadequacies and errors. The unfortunate truth is that the more you focus on past mistakes, the more likely you are to repeat them. Remember the good stuff, learn from the bad, and move on from the rest.

The world is interested in who you are *right now*. This moment. If your past does catch up with you and others see you only for what or who you *were* rather than who you are, it is your responsibility to show them otherwise. You can only do this by building, creating and living your best future.

Your future is present

It is important that the decisions you make are based on a sound knowledge of what your values are and what you want in life. The decisions you make (or neglect to make) determine what you will be, do and have in the future. What follows is a thought experiment designed to help you understand what you truly value in and about your life. The results might surprise you.

Oily beam test

Imagine you and I are standing at opposite ends of an empty room, approximately ten metres apart. Starting at your end and ending at mine, I draw two parallel lines about half a metre apart. I say to you that if you can walk between the two lines towards me you can have the £10 in my hand. No tricks. All you need do is walk. Would you do it? Probably.

Next, we put two chairs in the room, one at your end of the room and the other at mine. Then get a very strong piece of wood, ten metres long and half a metre wide. Secure each end on either chair. I stand at one end, you at the other. If you walk along the plank, without falling, you can have the £20 I have in my hand. No risk, no danger.

Now imagine you are out of the room. Think of two very tall buildings in a city that you know. We are on top of them, standing at least 50 storeys high. You are on one and I am on the other. A steel 'I' or 'H' beam about half a metre wide is placed between the buildings and is bolted securely at each end. I invite you to walk along the beam. You have to walk upright, and you have to stay on the beam. If you were to fall off you would very probably die. Would you do it for £50? Would you do it for £500 or £5,000? How much would I have to offer before you would cross that beam? A million? Ten million? Not at all?

Let's complicate it now. It has suddenly become dark. The wind is gusting. It is beginning to rain. There is a fine film of oil on the beam. Now, you have to cross the oily, wet beam in windy conditions, remaining upright. Would you do it? For £50, £5,000, £5 million, £20 million? Or would all the money in the world not tempt you?

Now, take a moment to think about the *really* important things in your life: family, friends, careers, homes, possessions, dreams.

So you are on the top of the building, I am on the other. The wet, oily beam is between us. The wind is blowing. I have a large bag in each of my hands. The two things you value most highly are in those bags. You have 30 seconds to cross the beam or one is taken away from you forever. *I* get to choose which one. Would you cross?

Go through your list. Imagine that I am holding your family in one hand and your friends in the other. Which would you choose? Imagine I have your career in one hand and your family in the other. Which would you choose? Imagine I have your career in one hand and your dreams in another. Which would you choose? Imagine I have your dream job in one hand and your home in another. Which would you choose? As you go through your list, you will be able to organize your values in a way that shows you what is most or least important in your life. When you build your future, consider your values. Remind yourself what is important to you. Stick to those and you cannot go far wrong.

Making the plan and creating your future

You know what you value. You know what has to change. You know what you want your future to look like and who you want in it. It is time to build a vision and make a plan. A different life doesn't just happen. As we talked about at the start of this chapter, the past and present are going to try to interrupt and interfere. The plan you make has to take into account where you are now.

Review the information you have generated throughout this chapter and make a list of what is good about your life, what you would like to change, and what you have to do to make the change.

Dreams to reality in eight steps

In Chapter 1 we said that there is no single recipe for a good life, nor are there eight magical steps to a great future, but there are a few guidelines …

The answers to these questions will help you construct an actionable plan.

◆ Dream to vision – What do you want to happen?

◆ Vision to reality – What has to happen to get you there?

- What skills do you already have?

- What skills do you need to acquire?

- What challenges might obstruct your progress?

- What are the solutions to the challenges?

- Actions – What exactly do you have to do first, second, third … to achieve your vision?

In sales training, there is a technique called the broken record that is also useful if you want your money back from a disgruntled shop assistant. The technique requires you to repeat what you want regardless of what objections the other party has. When I was first learning to put this technique into practice, I took back a faulty toaster. I didn't want a replacement, I wanted my money back. The sales assistant was reluctant and unco-operative to say the least. So I dug my heels in and ignored everything he said to me and repeated, 'I want my money back … I want my money back … I want my money back …'. Eventually, I felt a gentle shake on my shoulder and bringing me out of my trance, the managing director of the shop, who had been brought to the scene, said politely, 'Excuse me sir, you were given your money back five minutes ago.'

So, that leads me to number eight: how will you know when you get there?

Your plan can be short-, medium- or long-term. Some people say that you cannot plan more than one year ahead because you don't know what is going to happen any further ahead than that. However, planning is *designed* to make sure that you *do* know what you intend to happen, and that you can influence events. If you have a plan, you will be in a better position to manage future surprises instead of waiting for them to happen and hoping they won't derail you.

Imagine you were planning the next ten years of your life. What do you want to be, do or have in ten years?

To make this easier, break your plan into the following times:

- Ten years

- Five years

- Three years

- Two years

- One year

- Six months

- Three months

- One month

- Tomorrow

What do you have to do *tomorrow* to make sure you achieve your vision in ten years?

Vision-planning tool

There are thousands of business tools on the market that are designed for making life easier. The best tool I have ever used is a Gantt chart, named after the creator.

A Gantt chart is a project-planning tool. It provides you with a visual image of the activities you have to complete for the project to be a success, when you have to complete them by, what activities are taking place simultaneously, and who is involved in the activity.

It is an ideal way of turning your dream into reality. It allows you to manage your events and monitor your progress.

Using a Gantt chart to plot your dream

The following is a sample Gantt chart:

VISION

Month/ Week/Day	October 2001										
	1	2	3	4	5	6	7	8	9	...	
Activity 1	x	x	x	x	x						
2			x	x	x	x	x				
3		x									
4							x	x	x	x	
5									x	x	
6									x	x	
7											
8											
9		x						x			
10											
...											

1   Write your vision or goal at the top of the page.

2   Insert the timing across the top of the grid. Is the goal going to be achieved over days, weeks or months?

3   In the activities column, write down everything you have to do to achieve the goal. Do this in as much detail as makes sense to you. Include phone calls, mailings, meetings, books to read, everything.

4   Determine what you are going to do and when. Build the plan. Remember to be realistic. What other commitments do you have? How much can you really achieve in one day? If you give yourself too much to do, you will become frustrated. Too little and you will lose focus. Build the plan in pencil so that you can make changes. Later, you can progress to a computerized planning system if it makes sense to do so.

Top ten tips on your past, present and future to think about

1   Life is not meant to be difficult.

2   For each minute of work you do, have two minutes of fun.

3   Don't wait until you retire to explore the world.

4   Let others be responsible for themselves.

5   Love yourself and be good to yourself *first* (but not at the expense of others).

6   Have at least one new experience every day, one adventure every week, and a true surprise once a month.

7   Let people around you be their best.

8   Don't take it personally if people let you down.

9   Spend some time alone.

10 Appreciate the planet and everything in it, *always*.

Final thought

If you can imagine it, you can do it. Imagination is limitless.

A caution. First, do no harm. Second, think through the consequences.

06

chapter six
mental space makes money

If your finances are in disarray, you will be distracted subconsciously – and sometimes consciously – before you even begin your daily activities, whether at work or leisure. It's one of the biggest barriers to having mental space. From when the mail arrives in the morning, through to when you pay for dinner at night. Have you ever had that feeling of doom when you offer your credit card? Will it be refused? Images of the supermarket queue built up behind you, the cashier tells you the card has been declined. Run? Make an excuse? Leave? Write a cheque? Would they even take a cheque? Fear, frustration, embarrassment …

Are you in the habit of ignoring your finances and hoping that somehow they will have magically put themselves in order?

No news is not always good news as far as money is concerned. When the crunches (plural) come, they will not be as easy to sort as they would if you had been taking care of business as you went along.

Without referring to any bank or credit card statements, get a piece of paper and write on it:

◆ The names of *all* debit, credit and store cards you have, along with:
  – their current balance;
  – the exact date that the next payment is due on each;
  – how much will be going out of your bank account.

- All direct debits or standing orders on your bank account, including:
  - how much each is for;
  - when they are due out.

- Your bank balances, along with:
  - the dates of the next income(s);
  - the amounts of the next income(s).

When you have done that, get all your latest bank, credit and store card statements. Check how accurate you were.

Could you do it? How close were you? Did you not even start because you didn't have the information in your head?

Fear about money only exists when you don't have the facts.

If your finances are in order, life is a whole lot easier. There is a very good reason why money is called currency – if you have it you are *current*. If your finances are in order, you can do what you choose to do or need to do free from stress or worry.

There is only one reason why people have money problems – they spend more each month than they bring in. Gradually, debt builds up to a level where the debt prevents any possibility of paying it off, resulting in people becoming trapped in debt-payment systems that charge massive interest and never allow them to clear the debt fully. For most of those unfortunate enough to be in this position, their finances look something like this:

Unexpected expenses

Tax and government requests for your money (gone before you get your pay cheque)

Debt repayment

Utility, home, food and transport costs

PLUS

Luxuries, mostly bought on credit ... to be added to debt repayment next month

Ideal scenario: clear the debt, legally reduce the tax burden, allow for unexpected expenses (for instance, vehicle repairs), get the best deals on your general living expenses, and learn how to make your money work for you. This chapter is *not* a comprehensive guide on how to get financially sorted; there are several superb books on the subject listed in the resource section. What this chapter will do is help you clear your head about your money so you can start to clear it for real. It might give you a much-needed jolt that will get you off your backside and moving towards a genuinely secure financial future.

If, after you have sorted your finances, you find you don't have any money, you will still be better off because you will know how much you *don't* have, and you will then be much more likely to do something about it.

Emotional money

Do this *before* you read any further ...

◆ Get out your wallet / purse or whatever you keep your money in.

- Take out the note of the highest value / denomination.

- Now, tear it in half.

Have you done it yet? Have you torn it in half? Are you still holding onto it in one piece, saying 'No chance!'?

What are you feeling at the moment? What's going on in your mind? Are you thinking about the value of the currency you are holding and that if you tore it in half you would lose it? Or did you wait until you realized that you could tear it in half because a piece of tape would put it back in one piece again and make it money again instead of scrap paper?

If tearing that note in half was difficult, imagine what you are doing with money anyway: paying an insurance policy that is worth nothing by the time you want to cash it in (tearing money in half); buying things you never use (tearing money in half); paying more than you should for something because you can't be bothered to look for a better deal (tearing money in half).

We put a lot of emotion into money. Losing it upsets us.

Not being paid enough agitates us. Being paid too much worries us. Having it makes us feel safe and secure. Not having it makes us feel frightened and 'not current'. Ironically, not having it can make us feel that we will remain part of something – 'Everyone has money problems and if I have plenty of money, how will my friends / family feel around me?' How often have we heard about lottery winners losing everything within a year or a few months of winning millions? Is it because they don't know how to manage money if they've never had it before? Or is it because it's safer to be like everyone else and worry about not having enough money?

For some reason, the emotion we attach to money disappears as soon as it doesn't look like money any more.

mental space

momentum

Even credit cards manage to deceive you. Have you ever bought something to the value of £8, only to be told at the till that they only take credit cards for purchases over £10, so you pick up something you don't really need or want to make it £10 or more. You won't have to do that often for it to have an impact on your monthly cash flow. Besides, if you were paying cash and were told that you couldn't pay cash for anything less than £10, would you walk out of the shop? Would you think you were being manipulated and ripped off? Yes, you would. But, because plastic doesn't hold the same emotional value as cash, you are happy to let yourself be ripped off.

Education

We are the way we are about money primarily because we were never taught to be any other way. We were taught how to earn money – get an education, get a job, get a better education, get a better job; the better your job, the higher your salary, and so on. However, the higher your salary, the higher your taxes, the bigger your house, the greater the cost. People living in one-bedroom apartments can have more disposable income than those living in penthouses whose disposable income is often disposed of before they even get it. We are not taught how to make money work and we are not taught how to generate an income unless it involves working a full week. We are not taught that living is meant for learning and exploration and expansion, growth, excitement and passion. Instead, we are taught that if we have a good job and earn a good wage, then we are a success. Tosh!

There is so much more to life than just working to earn enough to pay taxes and bills.

Get your money in order and get your head straight about the value of money and how to make it work. It's much more fun.

Technology is designed for personal financial management. Instead of waiting for your statements to come through once a month, you can use the Internet for online banking and be fully informed any time, anywhere about your money.

Wealthy people don't just know how to *make* money, they know how to *spend* it and *manage* it.

Below is a strategy for getting your finances in order. If you do this, you will have *real* mental space. You will appreciate that money is far from being the root of all evil. The more you know about your money, the easier it is to make more. It is merely *currency*; the material that society uses to allow us to exchange goods and services. The more *current* you are, the more freely you can interact with society at large.

Perhaps more importantly, if you understand your finances, you will be much more confident, you will be less stressed, and each and every day you will experience less fear.

Learn about money

Learn how to manage money. Learn how to *make* it as opposed to just earning it. Learn how to spend it and invest it. Learn how to enjoy it. Before that, learn about your current financial position.

Knowing where your money goes

Even though it might seem like a big job, this exercise may be one of the most important you will ever do. Take time out and do it. You will be surprised by what you find. The insight will allow you to manage your expenditure with your eyes open.

◆ Gather your bank, store and credit card statements for the last 12 months (even if it costs you to get copies).

◆ Either on a computer or a piece of paper, create a table with columns breaking down exactly what goes out each month. Categorize the expenditures according to what they are, i.e. food, clothing, transport, taxes, heating, telephone and electricity bills, dinners out, entertainment, computers and technology, etc. Your table might look something like this:

Date	Food	Clothing	Home improvement	Car fuel	Bills
1 Jan	£24.30				
3 Jan	£95.10	£112.99		£34.00	
4 Jan			£329.00		£34.00

◆ Add up each category over the 12 months. For instance, what did you spend on clothing each month for the last year?

◆ To get an average expenditure per month through the year on a particular category, divide the number for that category by 12.

Do this thoroughly and honestly. If you avoid being truthful, you will deceive only yourself.

The reason for this exercise is that although you make a purchase in one month, if you buy on credit, you may pay for it for six months to four years later (*plus interest*). This impacts your cash flow by increasing monthly debt payments and decreasing disposable income and capital.

When a friend of mine did this exercise, he found that in that year he had spent an average of £1,200 per month on IT equipment (£14,400 in the year). Most of this was bought on credit, so the final pay-off was much higher because of very high interest! This included everything: printers, inks, consumables and other hardware. It did not include paper. He had no idea that so much income was going towards technology that simply seemed like a good idea at the time.

When he was aware of what he was spending his money on, he was able to reduce these outgoings and manage his expenditure more intelligently.

Tearing the note in half showed you how emotionally attached you are to money. You now also have a good idea of where it goes each month.

Open your eyes and clear your mind of money matters

Money problems are difficult to manage if you don't know what is going on. As hard as it may seem, make yourself aware of your financial situation. Get into the habit of reading and analyzing your bank and credit card statements *every month*.

Then:

1 Contact your bank and get a list of all the direct debits and standing orders you have on your accounts and check all of these outgoings against the actual bills.

> When we moved house two years ago, we didn't check all of the direct debits and found (a year later) that we had been paying the gas and electricity bill of the previous house all that time. The new owner of our home didn't complain (his bill was getting paid for him). The utility company was getting paid, so they didn't complain. Fortunately we got it all back. But we could have lost a lot of money.

2 Check all of the life and death insurance policies you have. Contact the company providing them and make sure that what you are paying over time makes financial sense.

> A colleague recently cancelled a policy that no amount of maths could make sensible. Each month he was paying £165 into the policy. He contacted the company for a redemption figure and was quoted £704.00 (he had been paying into the policy for two years). Two months later, he contacted the company again for an updated figure and the value of the policy value had gone up by £6. He had, in the mean time paid in £330! The policy would be fully

redeemable in another ten years and he would be getting (once all the fees and charges had been paid) less than what he had paid. This may be OK if the cover suits your needs and you are prepared to pay for it, but investments and policies are meant to be places where your money works (e.g. you pay £1 and get back £1.50 over time). The important thing is to be aware and make informed choices. Check your investments. Don't take for granted that because an independent financial advisor said it's a good deal, that it is. It's generally a good deal because the advisor gets the best commission from it. This may sound cynical, but it's reality. Learn the facts for yourself. Not everyone has your best interests in mind. Be responsible for your own money.

3 Check and fully understand *all* your bank charges and other fees the bank takes from your account every month. Banks do sometimes make mistakes: check that they are not overcharging you for anything.

4 Check all the purchases you make on credit. Some credit companies have higher interest rates than others. If you can, increase the payments each month or pay the 'expensive credit' off as early as you can. You will save a *lot* of interest.

Several years ago I bought a laptop and decided to pay it off over 12 months. The cost per month wasn't too much so I set up a direct debit and ignored it. Six months after the purchase, I received a letter from the credit company saying that I had the option of paying the rest of what was owed within so many days or the interest would be increased on the loan by £400. I didn't pay it off and the loan (and my monthly payments) increased. Three months later, I received another letter from the loan company saying that if I paid off the loan within seven days, I would save myself from paying the further £300 in interest that they were going to be putting on the loan if I kept it going for the full 12 months. What these companies count on is people not being able to pay, or being too financially lazy to organize their payments, and thus giving in and paying the full amount, including all the interest. Some years ago, 'inertia selling' was made illegal for things such as books. Perhaps this kind of inertia financial selling will also be made more difficult and perhaps illegal one day. Unfortunately, it is currently legal, and if I had read the small print I would have known about it, but I didn't. I paid the bill, second time around, and saved 12 months' interest.

5   Keep interest payments as low as possible by moving money between cards. Check the rate of interest on your credit cards. Most companies advertise a low interest rate for the first six months. Some offer an ongoing low interest rate even after the initial six months. If you have such a card, use it to keep down your interest.

6   If you automatically pay the full amount on each card every month, you should pay no interest at all.

7   Since credit card companies make money from your interest payments and other charges completely they are often reluctant to help you clear the balance each month and thus pay no interest at all. If you want to arrange this, and they will not let you do it, close that account and move to a new credit card company that will. Also, don't take for granted that because you have asked the credit card company to take the full amount each month that they will. In my experience, they seem to conveniently forget instructions like that and charge you the interest anyway.

If you want to be financially literate, then keeping a record of your finances is vital.

When you know exactly what your financial situation is, you will have two choices:

1   Adjust your way of life to fit your income, or

2   Adjust your income to fit your way of life.

Money and guilt

Have you ever been out with a group of friends for a meal and felt compelled to pay more than your fair share? The opposite is where everyone tries to avoid buying the first round, which is usually the most expensive since everyone will have one. It is also more likely that the round will come back to you before the night is out. When the precedent has been set, everyone feels obliged to get a round because someone has bought one for them. This is unfair for tee-totallers or light drinkers.

This social behaviour stems from our reluctance to talk about pounds and pennies. If everyone were to pay for their share they would have to discuss money. For most of us, it's easier to say, 'I'll get this' instead of, 'My share is £xx.yy'.

Instead of being socially bonding, this can lead to resentment and damaged friendships.

Starving guilt

Next time you are out in a group, say straightforwardly that you would prefer to pay for your own meal instead of an equal share. You can be diplomatic. Say that you might want something more expensive and don't want others to subsidize you. That allows you to choose what you want, enjoy your meal, stick to your budget and keep your friends.

When someone in a group offers to buy a round, thank them and tell them that you prefer to get your own. That will take you out of the 'loop'.

It won't be easy. There will be pressures to conform.

If you want to get a grip on your money, begin by not letting others spend it for you.

Top ten tips on mental space and money

1   Do not evade dealing with money issues.

2   When money is flowing well, don't get complacent.

3   Don't delay. Get cheques to the bank promptly.

4   Pay bills on time.

5   Become friendly with your bank manager and your local tax office.

6   Get a good accountant. Agree a fixed annual rate and pay in advance by standing order or direct debit. That allows you to speak to them whenever you need without fearing a bill each time you ask a question.

7   Be honest with yourself about your money.

8   Avoid the vicious cycle of 'maxing out' your cards, paying them off with a low-interest loan and then maxing them out again.

9   It's tempting to shop around for everything. But remember to weigh the difference between the value of your time and the amount you will save by looking for a bargain.

10   Cheapest is not always best!

Final thought

In dealing with money, you will make mistakes. When something goes wrong and it costs you, instead of getting angry, frustrated and fearful that it will happen again, learn from it. Provided you *do* learn from the situation, treat the cost as 'school fees' – paying for your education.

07

chapter seven
creating time with mental space

Time and events

If it seems that you don't have time for anything and are stressed as a result, it will certainly be worthwhile to review how you spend your time, and to determine whether the actual things that you do each day are consistent with your values (see Chapter 5). Sometimes, you can be pulled into doing what you think you should do instead of what you want to do (for example, allowing work to totally take over your life). The key to remember with time management is that you have *choice.* The closer your activities are to your core values, the more rewarding the result will be.

Which seems better: choosing how much time you allocate to each event, or choosing what events you want to fill your time? Or is it a mix of both?

While you have no choice about how much time you have, you do have a choice about the events you fit into the time you have, which kind and how many of them. The following activity will help you identify which of your typical activities correspond to your values and will help you decide if you are spending your time well.

Make a pie chart using the blank circle below. Divide it into sections that show how you spend your available time (waking hours) during a typical week. If you want to, subdivide the work section with the categories of your work activities. You might want to get a more complete picture of the week. Account for all 168 hours by including sleep times. The completed pie might look something like this:

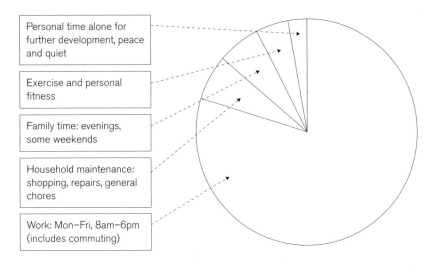

Personal time alone for further development, peace and quiet

Exercise and personal fitness

Family time: evenings, some weekends

Household maintenance: shopping, repairs, general chores

Work: Mon–Fri, 8am–6pm (includes commuting)

Now, build your own. This chart should represent how you presently spend your time during a typical week.

When you have completed your chart, return to the oily beam test outlined in Chapter 5. Place each activity or category of activities on which you presently spend your time on the beam to determine what is really important to you.

Now divide the circle below in a way that represents how you would prefer to spend your time based on your values. Compare this chart with the previous one and notice the differences.

Unless you are doing your ideal job and your life is balanced, the two charts will probably be different. It might be impossible to live your ideal life immediately, but it is possible to begin to change what you do during a typical week to begin to move towards your ideal. For instance, you might feel that you spend too much time at a desk at work and not enough time keeping fit. You may not be able to give up your job because you need the income, but you may be able to change the way you work to include some physical activity. Although it may not always seem like it, you do have a choice. You can always say *no*, you can say *yes*, you can say *maybe*. At work, at home, in everything you do, you have the choice.

Fitting life and dreams together

One of the most important things about time usage is reality. When you dream and plan, you can be as boundless as you like. When you act on your dreams, you need to be realistic. Your actions take place in the *real* world. It is important to know that you can achieve a great deal in a short amount of time if you manage your events carefully.

One of the American presidents said that if he had six hours to cut down a tree, he would spend five and a half hours sharpening the saw.

Planning and preparation is the key to event management.

Whether organizing your day or an entire project, the same principles apply:

◆ Decide what you want to do.

◆ Determine how much time you want to allocate to each act, task or vision.

◆ Plan as much detail as you can, including possible contingency plans.

◆ Take action, completing tasks as you go and updating your plan showing how accurate your original estimate was.

Four to six weeks at a time planning strategy for fitting it all in

If you have a demanding job and a full family life and still have other projects, it will take careful planning to make it all happen. I have used the system described below for many years. It works. Most people with full lives use some form of planning system. Many people only take into account their work activities, and wonder why the other aspects of their life seem neglected. This system accounts for *all* your time and *all* the events you want in your life.

◆ Review the post-oily beam test' pie chart allocating your time. Make a list of your different roles and projects, e.g. family, social, job-related, hobby, holiday plans, special projects, personal development, financial management, etc.

- Based on the future you want to create (developed in Chapter 5), determine the outcome you want to achieve for each item on the above list over a period of four to six weeks (I found four weeks was not quite long enough, while six weeks gave me time to do what I wanted).

- Allocate time for mental and physical holiday times (Quality Recovery Time, QRT – breaks and breathers).

- Next to each activity on the six-week list, jot in the approximate time you want to spend on the job and when you are going to do it. Write this in pencil because you will find that things change.

- Then, in your daily planning system (or whatever system you use), divide your day in half: work-related events and non-work-related events. In the to-do part of the planner, write in all the activities from your six-week list that are due to be done on that day. Make sure that you only put in what you can fit in to the time available. You will get it wrong to begin with. But you will learn. Quickly. And you will adapt the system to one that works for you.

For example, my most recent six-week plan looks something like this (not fully inclusive):

Role/project	Timing
Date: Mon 3 Sept–Sun 14 Oct **Evaluation:**	
Family:	
Email all family contacts with new email and www addresses for trip	3 Sept
Send Gran birthday card	10 Sept
Help Tania with prep for new job	10/11 Oct
Track books for Mum	3 Sept
Work/writing:	
Finish *Mental Space*	Deliver 10 Oct
Get articles in for *Business News* (Sept and Oct)	6 Oct
Social:	
Organize event with K&A	28 Sept
Email all social contacts with new email and www addresses for trip	10 Oct

Personal development:

Start learning French and Spanish for first leg of trip	13 Oct

Admin and financial management:

Finish all bank details	12 Oct
Fix direct debits for trip	12 Oct
Final accounts	12 Oct
Finalize policies	11 Oct

Special project (round-the-world cycle trip)

Tents and general equipment list from Calum	Collect 1 Oct
Collect bikes	9 Oct
Finish vaccinations	20 Sept
Decide on Europe or Australia	Ongoing
Almost ready to go	When ready

Health and fitness:

Daily walk/run	Daily
Daily cycle rides once bikes arrive	Daily
Get new coach for Aikido club	By 11 Oct

Evaluation

At the end of each week, month or six-week period, go back to your plans and evaluate how you did. Measure this by reviewing what you did during the period. Were you giving yourself too much or too little to do? Refer to your pie chart. How are you spending your time? What is not getting done? Does it really matter? Does it reflect your values? Are you getting everything done?

This system will help you ensure that you plan and design how you will achieve your dreams by carrying out concrete action to *make them happen*. Well-managed time means well-managed events within the time available.

Meetings and time

Meetings can be one of the biggest time wasters. A while back, I did quite a bit of work for one of the largest organizations in the world. One of my tasks was facilitating meetings. Often, I attended a meeting about which I was briefed only half an hour before. In effect,

mental space

momentum

I knew nothing about the content of the meeting (I was not a professional in the technical side of their business) but I did get to know the personalities of the people who attended. My job was to make sure that everything that was on the official agenda was discussed, dealt with and concluded. These meetings would sometimes last a full day. My biggest challenge was those people who decided that the meeting was a good way of getting out of work for a day. They would arrive, drink copious cups of coffee, catch up with friends, write up their own agenda and then make it their aim to disregard the official agenda in order to fit in their own idea of what should be covered.

The fact that I was not a professional in the subject matter was important, because I had no vested interest in what was being said (that was the job of the chair). I was concerned only with the *time* and *events*. As soon as someone's personal agenda started up, I had great delight in diplomatically but sometimes very firmly moving on with the formal agenda. Because I wasn't a part of the company and thus not tied up in the internal politics, no one objected when I broke their personal agendas. If they tried to object I would ask them (nicely) what relevance their point had to the agenda at hand. They often had to work hard to convince me and the rest of the group that it had any relevance at all. From my experience in facilitating meetings that lasted anything from a few hours to several days, here are a few tips on how to save time during meetings.

♦ Have a clear agenda agreed by all parties up front.

♦ When writing the agenda, have three categories of topics:
  – Topics that *have* to be discussed (vital and crucial).
  – Topics that *should* be discussed (important but not vital).
  – Any other business. Don't leave AOB to the end of the meeting. At the end of the day, people may be tired and (should be) wanting to get back to work. If there is too much AOB, the quality of discussion is not good, you will physically or mentally lose many of the attendees, and there will be no definite time limit because the AOB time is undefined. So, write the agenda, send it around and tell people to add any other business they want to include, then predetermine the time you

will allow for AOB. If it is not included before the meeting, it doesn't get discussed.

◆ At the start of the meeting, write up the exact agenda and the timing, e.g. points 1–4 before break one, points 5–7 before break two, etc.

◆ Start exactly on time. Don't recap for latecomers.

◆ Set and adhere to times for oxygen breaks.

◆ Take a break at least every 90 minutes.

◆ As the meeting progresses, cross off the subjects covered. Don't retrace your steps.

◆ When you are chairing or facilitating a meeting, the most important thing to do is prevent time wasters from taking over the agenda and waffling.

◆ Have someone take very clear and full notes. The person who takes the minutes should have some knowledge of the subject but should not be biased. The person who takes the notes should *not* be expected to contribute to the meeting.

◆ Always have a facilitator; it is their job to keep the meeting moving. If the meeting is going to be large and long, get someone from outside the company. The facilitator, like the minutes taker, cannot take part in the discussion. The facilitator must be assertive, firm and respected by those attending. Timing is the facilitator's number-one responsibility. If the meeting moves in such a way that it becomes clear that more discussion is needed, then it is the facilitator's responsibility to make any changes to the agenda to make sure the timing still works. The facilitator cannot be shy or shrinking. He or she must take control of the meeting from the very start.

◆ The chair is responsible for content although the facilitator can help with this. As soon as delegates begin to waffle or go off the subject, the chair (with the assistance of the facilitator) must get them back on the subject. Waffling is one of the great time wasters. Some people seem to make it their aim to speak rubbish at meetings. Make it clear, with a smile, at the beginning of the meeting that this will not be tolerated.

◆ Don't try to fit too much into any meeting.

◆ Don't run meetings for the sake of it. If you have a scheduled meeting every morning or every Friday, make sure there is a clearly understood, specific reason for it. Don't make meetings a habit.

◆ Full-day meetings are *never* as effective as those that last only a few hours. Keep them short and to the point.

◆ Don't invite known time wasters to meetings unless you can contain them or use their talents.

◆ Unless it is necessary, don't make meetings open to anyone who wants to come.

◆ Stop at the end of the meeting. The temptation is to carry it on in the halls outside the meeting. Once it's done, it's done.

◆ Make action come out of your meetings. Everyone must be clear about *what* exactly is to be done, *who* is to do it, *who* will follow up and *when* the follow-up will happen. People can be quick to agree to do something because it makes them look good; carrying it through is a different matter. The time spent carrying out actions arising from a meeting is more valuable than the time spent at the meeting.

◆ Don't waste anyone's time by creating senseless, unlimited or unallocated actions out of meetings.

Mental blocks and performance anxiety at meetings

Performance anxiety wastes time and an audience's patience. It can happen in any situation where you have to perform: contributing to meetings with colleagues, speaking on stage in front of several thousand strangers, or sitting an exam. Regardless of the context, the symptoms of performance anxiety may include clouded vision, blurred thinking, weak knees, excessive perspiration and weak lips to the extent that you think you would drool if you could summon up enough moisture. Then there is the activity, or lack of it, in your head: empty, full of babble, concern whether your zips and buttons are done, whether there is loo roll stuck to your shoe – take a step back, breathe and relax.

The main reason for this type of anxiety is that you are focusing on yourself and what your audience might be thinking about you, rather than what your audience needs and what you want to say to them.

Do not think about yourself – your audience doesn't really care about you. What they want is the *message*. You are merely delivering it. If you think about yourself, you will be preoccupied with stuff about which your audience has no interest. They want the message, then they want time and space to make decisions about it. They don't want to have to feel sorry for you. If that is what you want, then that is all you will get, and they will not listen to what you have to say.

Any time you have to perform, think only of your audience and delivering your message, and your anxiety will diminish instantly.

Speaking in meetings

During a meeting, it is easy to say the first thing that comes into your head instead of saying what you *mean* to say. It is equally easy to say nothing to avoid saying something stupid.

Keep your head clear during meetings. Most people have an agenda of their own and there are almost always internal politics. To respond successfully during meetings, generate mental space. These tips will help you:

◆ Think before you speak.

◆ As the meeting progresses, take notes to remind yourself of your thoughts.

◆ Don't be bullied into responding to comments or suggestions.

- Don't let anyone threaten you, emotionally, physically, intellectually or psychologically.

- Stick to the facts and don't get emotional.

Impromptu speeches in a hurry: seven steps in seven minutes

For most people, a prepared speech and contributing at meetings are easy compared with being asked to give an *impromptu* speech. One of two things may fill your mind when you are asked to speak with no notice: first, nothing at all, your mind goes totally blank; second, mental overdrive. To prevent either of these happening, relax and clear your head using one of the relaxation techniques discussed in Chapters 8 and 11. Then, use the following strategy to create a structure around which to build a clear and balanced speech.

1 Calm down, breathe and focus your mind on the specific topic you will be speaking about.

2 On a piece of paper, write the title of your speech in one clear sentence.

3 Either as a mind-map or linearly, write down three to six main topics you will want to cover during your speech (if you are being asked to speak without notice, it is unlikely you will have to speak for long, and four points are generally enough).

4 Write two sub-points for each of the main topics.

5 Briefly develop each point.

6 Write a conclusion.

7 Write an introduction.

Time and pressure

Learn to love it.

Controlled stress is healthy.

Trouble arises when you have too much to do and you are not in control of it. The more you plan, the more control you will have over events, and the less negative stress you are likely to experience. Balance out stress with recovery time. Take a break, finish work on time, and don't let activity obstruct your sleep. If you are tired, even the most simple events can become disasters.

Thinking time and purpose

You can spend days and days doing. But if you look closely at what you are doing, you might be surprised at how trivial most of it is. If you take time to consider what you want to do and how you want to do it, your time will have more purpose, and the events in your life will have more meaning. Some of the most important and valuable time is the time you take to think and reflect.

Finish-lines – a better word for deadlines

'Deadline' is a loaded word. It implies disaster if it isn't met. The interesting thing about deadlines is that often there are several attached to most large projects: the one stated at the start of the project, the one you impose on yourself, the one others impose on you, the real one and the delayed one. Be flexible and realistic, and if more time becomes available to complete a project, then use it.

What's the big deal about being late?

There is a difference between agreeing to extend a deadline and being late. If you are late, you are wasting someone else's time: that is disrespectful. Sometimes, it can't be helped, but let people know. Henry Ford said: 'Never complain, never explain.' If you are late, the person you are keeping waiting doesn't need to know all the intimate details of why you are late (unless it relates to them), and they most certainly don't need a made-up excuse. Keep it simple, keep it honest and don't make a habit of it. Being late all the time will only help you to develop a reputation for unreliability. Lateness increases stress for all involved. If you cancel all your other new year resolutions, try to make this one stick: be on time.

Top ten tips on time

1 As far as possible, do one thing at a time.

2 Work towards completion. Finish what you start before moving on to the next project or task.

3 Allow for some slack for unpredictable eventualities.

4 Rushing wastes time: relax.

5 Set realistic deadlines and adapt as the unknowable and unpredictable happen.

6 Be clear about how much of your time you can allocate to others.

7 Be present on the task you are doing: don't let your mind wander.

8 Make a written plan of events and actions needed to make them happen.

9 Make sure that those who need to know about your plans are kept well informed of any changes.

10 Allow for thinking time.

Final thought

Sometimes the best way to ensure you do everything you want to do in the time you have available is to take a break and evaluate your progress. Speed and action aren't always appropriate: stop and think.

chapter eight
perception: the world around you

It's all in your head

The world is what it is, madness, aggression, peace, harmony, contradictions, differences … It is your *perception* that determines whether it is chaos and disorder or sense and order. Think of a busy airport, people rushing everywhere, bumping and complaining, looking lost and bewildered. It's hot, your bags are heavy, everything is chaos. You become tense, and before you know it, you would rather you weren't going to an exotic island. Step back for a second. Take a look at the scene. Don't try to push and shove your way through people. Take your time, breathe and relax. See the events as they are. It's just a busy airport. Your mood begins to change, people seem to smile more. Anticipation replaces frustration. In a moment, chaos becomes excitement and fun. Airports are starting points of adventure. For the most part, they are exciting places. A change in perspective allows you to experience a different world, one free from anger, frustration, fear and debilitating tension.

Most anger and frustration comes from not accepting the world as it is.

Consider another example. Wars are fought because two sides have different views of who is right and who is wrong. People inflict horrific acts on each other believing they are perfectly justified and right in doing so. Understanding that what is terrorism to one cultural viewpoint is the justified action of a freedom fighter to another does not condone inhumanity. How do you persuade one side to acknowledge and appreciate the sentiments of the other? Our perceptions are not only ingrained in our conscious thoughts, they manifest in unconscious behaviours handed down from generations of behaviour and belief and adopted as 'normal' in a specific cultural context.

Mental space allows you to change some of your ingrained thinking.

You have the opportunity to consider someone else's perspective before making a judgement. It also means that you have the skills required to stop, slow down, change your perspective and see things in a more constructive light when stress and negative responses to a situation are simply making matters worse.

Practice perspective

This exercise can be done wherever you have some time just to play: sitting at a bus stop, having a cup of tea or attending a meeting that is uninteresting. Notice an event or activity going on around you. Imagine you were involved. How would you manage it? Next, imagine you were one of the people involved in the event, or a world leader or someone else entirely. How would you manage that event if you were someone else? Step into their shoes, think of what these different people would have to consider in responding to the event. What would you bring to the event that they could not?

Look for reasons why the event should or should not be taking place. Look for reasons why each person might be right or wrong. Look for justification for each person's actions. Look at the event from every perspective possible. Practise this often, play with it and take it seriously when you are in a position of conflict.

Two important notes to remember:

◆ Although you might be able to understand or even appreciate another person's perspective, you don't necessarily have to agree.

◆ A person's actions *always, always, always* make perfect sense to them at the time.

Stress happens either when a situation outweighs your perceived ability to deal with it or, worse, when you are overloaded without realizing it.

This perception may vary from day to day, moment to moment. *Perception* is the operative word. You might have no more to do on Tuesday than you had on Monday, but because your mood or environment is different, what you have to do might seem more than it really is, and the perception that you cannot cope may increase regardless of the reality of your current surroundings.

Thought experiment

Think of a busy main street you are familiar with. Imagine two people walking along that street. Both see the same street, same people, same events. A bus narrowly misses a cyclist, someone gets her bag snatched, a couple is fighting, a child is crying … At the end of the street, one of your imaginary pedestrians might be tense and frustrated and the other will shrug and say, 'That's life.' The very next day, the same two people walk down the same street. This time, their reactions are reversed. The one who felt quite relaxed the day before notices exactly the same events and this time they are upset by them. The person who was agitated the day before doesn't respond at all.

Stress is created by the way you respond to a situation rather than the situation itself. In a potentially stressful environment, instead of focusing on how not to get stressed by it, focus on how you can deal with it and improve it or, if you cannot change it, what has to become true within you for you to accept it.

A number of stressors can affect your ability to perceive the world in a calm, balanced way:

Environment – noise, chaos and pollution.

Social – people, deadlines, financial problems.

Physiological – aches, pains, poor nutrition, lack of exercise.

By far the most dominant and potentially damaging are *your own thoughts*. As Shakespeare said, 'There is nothing so good or bad except thinking makes it so.'

In many stressful situations, we want to act instinctively and either run or fight, but often we can do neither. The physiological damage occurs when we must be still and smile while experiencing inner fury.

Re-interpreting stress

For thousands of years, doctors have known about psychosomatic illness. *Psyche* (the mind) can make *soma* (the body) sick in many different ways. As a result of the stress of witnessing or being a victim of a serious incident, symptoms may develop in addition to any direct injury.

The symptoms might be physical, emotional or mental.

Whether stress is chronic or acute, extreme or mild, it can cause illness – more so in some than others, and some people seem not to be affected at all.

Symptoms may take some time to develop to the level sufficient for diagnosis. By then, the illness may be difficult to treat. Headaches, high blood pressure, digestion, skin, breathing … all systems of the body are susceptible.

Negative interpretations of everyday events and habitual feelings, emotions and thoughts that are consistent with those perceptions often result in physical or mental illness. Behaviour arising from a negative view of the world affects the wellbeing of others too.

A response that may have been appropriate for the original event in that context, at that time, might not be appropriate now, particularly

mental space

if it has developed into a habit that does not suit changed circumstances.

Take a break

Two hormones that are important in the regulation of your basic activity and rest cycles are cortisol and beta-endorphin. Cortisol, which rouses you to action, has a decay time of approximately 90–120 minutes. At the end of this time, after expending energy, you might naturally yawn, lapse in attention, start making mistakes, or find it difficult to concentrate. You might even feel a little tired. As the cortisol decays, the beta-endorphin cycle begins. This lasts for typically 14–22 minutes and helps you to rest and relax while your body naturally recovers – provided that you do actually rest. As you begin to recover, more cortisol is released, which arouses you to a further activity cycle. This alternating pattern of activity and rest continues throughout the day. Between 3 and 5 pm, a particularly deep rest period is demanded by the body. This was termed 'the breaking point' by Japanese researchers who worked in this field during the 1980s. Some counties have built this rest period into their cultures. For example, traditionally in Spain there is a siesta, during which shops and businesses close while people rest.

Problems arise when you override the signal to rest using stimulants like tea, coffee or sugar, or even just ignoring it, which encourages the body to suppress it habitually. The cortisol and beta-endorphin still act as described above.

Overriding these signals can lead to a wide variety of physical, mental and emotional symptoms. These include sleep disorders, an inability to concentrate and agitation.

It's not necessary to take your sleeping mat to the office and roll it out every couple of hours for a little snooze on the floor. A short rest could mean stretching your legs for a few minutes, having a drink of water, eating a little protein, going for a walk or making a short social visit. Please do not smoke. Apart from the stimulating affect of nicotine, cigarettes contain several thousand toxins. One teaspoon of nicotine is enough to kill a horse. The amount of tar is specified on the box. Also, avoid caffeinated tea and coffee. For information on the effects caffeine has on your body, see Chris Fenn's book, *The Energy Advantage*, (details in the resource section).

If you do override the rest periods regularly, you may find that at the end of the day you are unable to relax properly and have to resort to alcohol, which is a depressant. The long-term affects of this are only predictable in the sense that some system or other in your body will suffer – it is impossible to predict which one.

All of the above material is covered in great detail in two texts by Ernest Rossi: *Psychobiology of Mind Body Healing* and *The 20 Minute Break*. For details of both books, see the resource section.

Carrot or stick

One way to encourage yourself to keep your mind open and your perspectives clear is to reward yourself. If you work in a conventional environment, you may not feel fully recognized or rewarded for your efforts. Instead of waiting for a reward from someone else, take responsibility: reward yourself. Determine what you are going to accomplish and what your rewards will be (*not* sweets, sugars, salt or flour, as this only rewards the taste buds). Vary your rewards. Choose things that are good for you, things you really want: anything ranging from an evening in a steam room to a proper holiday for finishing a big project on time. Have plenty of reasons to treat yourself. You will feel happier, your motivation will increase, and your stress levels will reduce.

Anti-ostrich policy

Maintain an anti-ostrich policy. Being open minded and receptive to new ideas will make your day more creative and problem free. If you avoid putting your head in the sand, you will be aware of what is going on around you: potential problems and their solutions. Potential problems only become real and unmanageable when they are ignored. Keep your head out of the sand and your mind open. When you no longer fear managing difficult issues, they won't seem so big. Fear of problems makes them worse. Treat problems as a series of events that you have to disentangle.

A word of warning: 'hyper-vigilance' can be just as damaging as 'hypo-vigilance'.

mental space

Rid yourself of clutter and confusion

An environment you can and must control is your workspace. Every piece of paper that sits on your desk attracts your attention several times a day. If each had a sonic deadline, you would have a desk covered in alarm clocks sounding off every few minutes alerting you to the pressure you are under, interrupting your concentration, inducing chronic stress, causing physiological damage, and reducing your capacity to concentrate.

If you have a clear desk, your environment will look and feel in control and the perception that your environment is out of control will diminish. You may have a great deal to do, but you will be able to tackle each task one at a time with a clear mind.

Real people

A delegate at one of my workshops had a novel method of dealing with clutter. He would place all the general mail into one pile in a tray in the corner. If he needed something, he would take it out of the pile, work on it and then file it or place it on top of the pile, but only if he knew he would need it again. Gradually, documents that he did not need and did not have to read would work their way to the bottom of the pile. Every three months, he would throw away the bottom half of the pile without looking at it.

His argument was that if he did not need something in three months, he would not need it at all, and if it really was important, then someone would have sent him another copy and the new copy would be in the top half of the pile.

His business is extraordinarily successful. Since he adopted this strategy, he has quartered the volume of reading he does. People know that if they want him to pay attention to something, they must take the time to speak to him. As a result, his desk and his mind are clear. Always.

Your living space

Your living space is a reflection of your mind and your thinking processes. Compare the state of your home and the state of your mind. If your home is immaculate and organized to the degree that one of your main tasks each day is to make sure that everything is always in its place, it does not mean that your thinking is predictable and unimaginative. If your home is a pile or chaos, it does not necessarily mean that your thinking is disorganized. If your home is messy but organized, it does not automatically mean that you are creative but distracted.

At this point, don't fall into the body language trap – if someone scratches their nose it does not necessarily mean they are lying. They might just have an itchy nose.

The only relation between your home and mental space is comfort.

If you are happy with your living space, if you love going home, if you feel calm and peaceful, creative and relaxed in your living space, then your living space is right for you. If, on the other hand, you spend most of your time out because every time you go home you are reminded of chores you don't want to do, then it may be worth taking time to organize and clear your space so that you can live in it, rather than use your creative ability to generate excuses on how to avoid it.

The space you live in should be the one place in the world where *you* can just be. If you have a big, chaotic family, make sure you have at least one space and one time that is yours.

Reduce stress and increase mental space and perspective

Breathing

Although most of your brain cells would die without oxygen within three to five minutes, you can live a whole lifetime without breathing *properly* and not be aware of it. Your body uses your breathing as a signal to tell you when something is wrong: when you are stressed or threatened you feel it in your breathing. When you are tired, you yawn to take in more air. When you are in a room with poor ventilation, it doesn't take long before you feel uneasy, get a headache or feel tired. These signals should not be ignored.

Correct breathing can relieve a number of symptoms, including stiffness, tension, irritability, headaches, fatigue and depression. Poor breathing habits affect your ability to monitor stress and to respond positively to events around you.

The following breathing exercises don't take long to do. You can do them anywhere. The exercises don't take long to learn and they will help reduce stress. Practise some kind of breathing exercise several times every day if you can. Teach yourself to notice how your breathing responds to different types of events. Gradually, this will become routine. When you are in a difficult situation, such breathing techniques will help you respond calmly.

When you are faced with a challenging situation, an open mind and a shift in perspective may help your body learn to relax naturally.

Use this first breathing exercise if you don't want others around you to know you are practising. At each in-breath, make sure you are breathing into your abdomen rather than your chest. To check this (assuming you can't place your hands on your abdomen area to check whether it is moving or not), place your awareness around your waist and as you breathe your should feel a tightening around your clothing.

◆ Exhale comfortably and take in a slow, deep breath and hold for a slow count of at least four.

◆ Slowly exhale.

◆ Take three or four breaths like this and relax.

If you have only a few minutes, this yoga breathing exercise is wonderful for *relaxing* and *focusing*:

◆ Close your eyes for a few moments.

◆ Place your right thumb on your right nostril and block it.

- Breathe in deeply and slowly through your left nostril for four seconds.

- Block both nostrils using your thumb and your right middle finger and hold for four seconds.

- Remove your thumb from your right nostril and slowly exhale.

- Pause for four seconds.

- Then continue by breathing in through your right nostril, closing both, and exhaling through your left.

- Continue for as long as you feel comfortable.

If you are tired and you have much to do, this exercise will help *wake you up* and *increase alertness*:

- Stand or sit up straight.

- Breathe abdominally.

- Hold your breath for a count of six.

- Purse your lips and blow out short bursts of air fairly forcefully until you have totally exhaled.

- Breathe in deeply again and repeat the exercise several times.

Be careful not to make yourself dizzy. If you do, stop.

Being present and in perspective

It is impossible (and undesirable) to be totally focused and present all the time. Imagination and creativity happen when your mind wanders beyond your present space and time. Sometimes, however, you need to be fully present and aware. This exercise will help you develop the necessary state of mind:

- Sit or stand still for a moment.

◆ First, close your eyes if you can, and notice what you can hear. How many conversations can you make out? What are people saying? Can you hear any traffic? What is the furthest sound you can hear? What is the closest sound you can hear? What is the most familiar or the most foreign or unusual sound? What is the most or least pleasant sound? Describe every sound you can hear.

◆ Next, notice what you can feel. How close are people to you? What does the floor feel like beneath your feet? What do your clothes feel like on you? Is there a breeze? If so, what direction is it coming from?

◆ With your eyes open, notice the colours. How many different shades of red or blue or orange can you see? What is the most common colour in your view? What is the least common colour? Now notice the shapes. If you observed your surroundings and had to describe them in terms of shapes only, and not what the objects really are, how would you describe them?

◆ Finally, appreciate your surroundings.

No matter how noisy or chaotic your present surroundings, when you *really* pay attention and are present, you will be surprised at the level of comfort and relaxation you experience. This may simply be the result of knowing your surroundings for what they are instead of making interpretations.

Do this as often as you have time, especially when you feel that your environment might be beginning to get out of control.

> **Top five tips on keeping your perception of the world in perspective**
>
> 1   Keep to the facts and keep an open mind.
>
> 2   Remember that people's actions always make sense to them. If you want to understand people and their actions, be politely curious and ask.
>
> 3   Be prepared to admit you are wrong and make appropriate changes.
>
> 4   Chaos is merely a collection of conflicting events.
>
> 5   Life doesn't have to be a tragedy.

Final thought

Try this thought experiment or, provided you take sensible precautions, do it for real. You will need a group of people, a thermometer, and three buckets of water: one very cold (almost freezing), another at room temperature (around 20°C), and a third at about the temperature of the hottest bath you can safely tolerate. Each of you take turns: sit for a *short* time with your left hand in the cold water at the same time as your right hand is in the hot water, then put both hands into the room-temperature water. You will notice that, although both hands are now immersed at the same temperature, the left hand feels that it is in hot water, while the right feels that it is in cold water. This can be used as an allegory to show how different people will interpret the same environment in entirely different ways.

Your memories, experiences and attitudes build a mental model of the world that act as filters on incoming information. Your senses – sight, hearing, touch – absorb *everything*. As new information passes through your senses into your brain, you make sense of it by fitting the information into your mental model. This filtering process means that instead of seeing the *real* world, you base your knowledge of the world on your interpretations of it.

chapter nine
self-concept

What determines how people view you is not what you look like, who you know or what you wear; it is self-concept. If you consider yourself to be clever, talented, healthy, fit and active, you will behave in a way that is consistent with that self-concept and so reinforce it. Similarly, if you believe you are unattractive or inadequate, you will behave in a way that projects those beliefs about yourself. Other people might not be able to read your mind, but they *can* (and do) read your behaviours.

If you want the world to treat you in a particular way, you need to be responsible for behaving towards the world so that you attract the responses you want.

You may have heard the truism, 'The meaning of your communication is the response you get.' Your self-concept is your communication to the world. The response you get from those around you is determined by your self-concept. Your self-concept starts in your mind.

Two people could have the same family backgrounds, jobs, physical qualities and interests, but their attitudes and self-concepts will determine how people see them. A school I went to was attended by an identical set of twins. Although they were physically identical, one had a brighter, more daring attitude to life. This was the difference that made it possible for the world and their classmates to tell them apart. The twin with a stronger self-concept would walk a little more upright than the other, speak a little more briskly, and smile more. She had a broader social life, took more risks, had more confidence, looked people in the eye, and voiced her opinions. The other spent more time alone. She was more introspective, behaved more according to what was expected of her, and tended not to say anything until she was able to agree with someone. These two physically identical people were distinguishable only by their self-concepts. They had different physical and verbal languages and vastly contrasting behaviour. Just like every other individual on the planet.

Self-concept: past, present and future

This thought experiment is a summary of a psychology undergraduate experiment.

◆ Cast your mind back to when you were 15 years old. What was your self-concept at the time? How did you perceive yourself then?

◆ Next, recall what you imagined you would be like *now* (at your present age).

◆ Put that aside for the moment, and consider what your concept of yourself is at the moment.

◆ What is the difference between your present self-concept and the one you imagined when you were 15 years old?

◆ When you have done that, imagine what you want your self-concept to be like in ten or 15 years time. How do you want to be in the future?

◆ Consider the gap between your present self-concept and what you want it to be in the future and decide what actions you need to take to close the gap.

Decide how you want to be treated

Before you can establish what you have to do to get something, you first of all have to decide what you want. This applies to self-concept as much as it does to goals or achievements. If, for instance, you want people to value and respect your opinions, your opinions must be worthy of respect. How will you do that? How would you like to be treated at work, at home, at leisure or in social circles? Do you behave in a way that will encourage people to treat you that way?

When the message gets lost in translation

The Scottish poet, Robert Burns put it: 'O Lord, the giftie gie us, Tae see oorsels as ithers see us.' However, seeing yourself as others see you and behaving such that you prove them right is impossible; one person might see you as a geek, another might see you as an Einstein, one might hate you, another might love you. The only predictable thing is your opinion of yourself.

A true story

I started my first *real* job when I was 19 years old. Everything about it was new: the people, the hours, the environment … I didn't yet know how to respond appropriately. On my first day, the whole crew went to the pub. During the course of the evening, one individual seemed to be avoiding me. After several months of his blatant rudeness. I approached him and straightforwardly and politely asked him why he behaved in that way towards me. Without hesitation he said, 'I just don't like you,' then turned away and carried on with his work. I was taken aback. Something like that had never happened to me before. Since my job was in the theatre, I had seen so much back biting, that his blunt honesty was, in a way, strangely refreshing. After a while, I approached him again. I asked specifically what I had done that had made him feel that way. Apparently, during that evening in the pub, I leaned my elbow on his shoulder to make a point during a story. Due to his height, he didn't appreciate being used as a stage prop (something thespians take seriously). That single action led him to dislike me without further question. I apologized and from then on we respected each others' space and left each other alone.

On the night in question, I had been new, insecure and shy. He had taken my behaviour as arrogant and intrusive.

Sometimes, to hide a negative self-concept, we *act out* a persona that we hope will be appropriate to the situation.

This can, and often will, backfire.

It is simply not possible to behave such that everyone responds to you the way you want. There will always be some people with whom you just do not blend, no matter how hard you try. Accept this, and life will be much easier. Trying to behave so that you are acceptable to everyone is *chameleon behaviour* (see Chapter 15). If you adapt your behaviour to suit every person or group you meet, you could lose the essence of you.

If you haven't yet done the exercises in Chapter 5, do them now, especially the oily beam test. To develop a healthy self-concept, know your core personal values and be happy to defend them in a good-natured way when they are challenged. Know your values and be true to them.

Power of influence

Don't be too concerned about what you cannot change. Work within your realms of influence. The only person you really have any control over is *yourself*.

To attempt to control others is hard and sometimes dangerous work.

You have complete control of yourself. It might not feel like it, but you have total choice to be, do and have whatever you want. How you *manage* that determines the extent of your influence.

There is a difference between control and influence. The more confident and certain you are of yourself, the greater your *influence* will be. Influence implies choice that other people have. People everywhere are influenced everyday; some by celebrity, some by leadership. Our environment and the events that take place in it shape our thoughts. We all, consciously or unconsciously, choose our influences. Control, on the other hand, implies a *lack* of choice. When people discover they are being controlled, they will revolt. But only after they become aware of it and have enough information and courage to act appropriately.

Influence is real power. Control will *always* be fought against.

The people who become leaders are those with the strongest self-concepts. Have you ever watched someone performing and you *know* that you could do a better job? That person has the job because the job and all it entails are within *their* self-concept, not yours. Some seriously *un*talented people are huge successes in business, politics and show business. The difference between them and someone who has more talent but is not so successful, is self-concept. 'I'm better than she is' is not the issue. 'She's doing it and you're not' is the point. Again, the question arises 'What will (not would) have to become true …?'

If you want to achieve something, it has to be within your self-concept, you have to *believe* that you can do it. When you believe, your behaviour will change in a way that will encourage *other* people to believe in you. That is when you begin to develop the power of influence.

Top ten tips on developing self-concept

1 Know your values and be yourself.

2 Don't wait for a disaster to make you look at yourself and decide you can be great.

3 Stop trying to please everyone: it's impossible.

4 Aim to be a strong, positive influence for the good of all concerned.

5 Stand straight. Look people in the eye. Be sincere.

6 Don't take yourself too seriously. Feel free to laugh at yourself at any time.

7 Confidence will get you further than talent – but a little talent will help!

8 The more new experiences you have and the more you learn, the stronger your self-concept will be.

9 Welcome criticism as feedback. Take it as an opportunity to grow and become stronger.

10 Never try to undermine someone else's self-concept. Even if yours is feeling shaky.

Final thought

What you imagine yourself to be is what you will become.

chapter ten
mental space, aggression and conflict

When two values, opinions or objects want to inhabit the same space, they will conflict. Archimedes discovered in his bathtub that it couldn't be done.

Conflict can arise suddenly or gradually. Individuals or groups holding one view may feel they will lose if the opposition wins and, as conflict escalates, the real reasons are forgotten in animosity and emotion.

In a formal debate, the argument begins, 'This house believes …' once the opening speaker is finished, the opposing views are heard in the same house without interruption. This format allows conflicting views to be aired fully and safely.

Conflict may arise when one or both parties feel unsafe to voice dissent.

Conflict is all the more confusing when those immediately involved in it are not those who created the perpetuating conditions. Do you know anyone who is having difficulty at home who is also experiencing difficulty at work? Do they display more anger during particular incidents than seems reasonable? Are they overly sensitive? Are they accusatory or judgemental?

When dealing with conflict, it helps if you are clear about its structure, and how it comes about.

The anatomy of conflict: seven steps from threat to revenge

Threat ➜ Fear ➜ Agitation ➜ Anger ➜ Frustration ➜ Redressing the balance ➜ Revenge

1   Someone perceives some form of *threat* to their person or space, whether physical, emotional, intellectual, financial, spiritual, social or familial.

2   The threat generates a *fear of loss*. Fear is a basic emotion. The root of hatred and hostility. Wars start because of a fear that one ideology is going to overrun another; arguments begin because one person threatens to overrun another.

3   When someone anticipates loss, whether a way of life, respect, money, opportunity, or a favourite vase on a mantelpiece, fear turns to *agitation*. This tends to be the end of rational thought. The key question people ask themselves is, 'What should I do?' If those involved don't come up with and act upon a thinking solution, they will generate blinkered vision and respond to the situation in terms of *emotion* instead of thought. At this point, all rational behaviour and logic evaporate.

4   Next is *anger*. Changes in blood pressure, sweating, skin colour, raised voices, shaking, and heated words. Anger is high energy. Once it burns off, frustration steps in.

5   *Frustration* happens when someone doesn't know what to do or when they know what to do and want to do it, but they are prevented from doing it. For instance, if someone were to kick you in the shin, or offend, or hurt you in some way, your immediate response would likely be anger. If you could not *do* anything, you would then become frustrated: the world is not as you would like it to be.

6   What now becomes important is *redressing the balance*: somehow getting an 'emotional re-set'. When anger is spent and people understand their frustration with their inability to win, they tend to depress: to slow down and think.

mental space

momentum

7 With the focus no longer being on anger or frustration, the intent will now be to get back to 'normal'; the course of action is not always intended to be good for all. *Revenge* is the most common. The conflict becomes calculated and *purposeful*. Basic emotions have passed, and thinking, reason and logic return. The conflict is over. An entirely new phase emerges. It may be cold, calculating and patient. It might take years before it is spent. It won't stop until the job is done.

This process can take years or it can happen in a matter of seconds: road rage, desk rage, any rage. Your aim should be to stop conflict and resolve it before it gets to the final stage.

A true story

A friend told me this story about a business that was in trouble. Everyone in the company knew. Only the boss and his select few knew exactly how serious the trouble was. The boss went into my friend's office and started asking questions aggressively about the *value* of her work (step 1: he threatened her). He questioned her value and necessity as an employee (step 2: she began to feel a fear of the loss of her job and credibility). He then became insinuating (step 3: she began to feel agitated). He had an agenda that my colleague didn't know about. An expert manipulator, he twisted her responses to suit his purpose (step 4: she became angry). She didn't know what to do (step 5: she become frustrated), and she noticed herself displaying physical signs of anger and frustration: hot, sweating, flushed face, unable to argue calmly and coherently (she became embarrassed). After the heat of the frustration and embarrassment, she slowed down. She was able to think rationally. She recognized that she wouldn't win this battle and began to consider what agendas her boss might have. Now she had stopped to think. She had reached step 6. She was interested in redressing the balance and re-setting herself emotionally.

It was near the end of the day so she said quietly that she would think overnight about what he said and they would talk again in the morning. Since he felt he had won, he agreed. The next day, she and several others resigned. The boss had needed to get rid of people but didn't want to pay severance. If people resigned (rather than be made redundant), he wouldn't have to. He didn't have the courage to be honest so his hidden agenda was to get people to leave and have them think it was their idea rather than his manipulation and bullying. The conflict passed. The boss thought he had won. However, revenge is patient. Over the next few months, those who had been treated badly informed the Inland Revenue, clients and competitors of the company's unethical practices. The business closed. Shortly after, he was declared bankrupt.

This story illustrates one possible route to 'emotional justice'. All parties recovered and got on with their lives, except the boss.

There are other, better ways to resolve situations of this nature. Although my friend could not have changed her boss's manipulating and subtly aggressive intent or behaviour, she could have responded such that she didn't get as hurt as she did at the start of the conflict. When conflict arises, it is important to *manage yourself*. You may not be able to control how other people behave, but you can control how you respond.

Breaking the conflict loop

In a conflict, *you* are the one experiencing *your* emotions. You cannot know what another person is feeling unless you *both* communicate, share and *have willingness*. Even then, you will only be able to understand their feelings in terms you are familiar with.

Most conflicts would not escalate into physical aggression if both sides could be shown a solution. The problem usually only follows when people cannot see a way forward in which both sides are able to retain their self-concept. Damage the self-concept of others at your peril.

In conflict, most people don't actually *think*. Not surprising since it is physiologically difficult. You think rationally with one part of your brain (the cortex) and 'emote' (to use one of Alfred Hitchcock's favourite words) with another (the limbic system). When threatened, frightened or angry, you 'emote'.

When you develop your mental space, you have an advantage. You are more able to manage competently threat, fear, agitation, anger and frustration.

There is a school of thought that asserts that people are responsible for their *own* feelings and nobody else's. If we lived in a perfect world, there would be some truth in this. We *are* responsible for the effects that our actions have on others. It is rude and irresponsible to think that you can say and do what you like with no regard for how other people might feel. It is worse to justify yourself by saying that if they are hurt by what you say, then they choose to feel that way and it's their responsibility. It is callous, stupid and disrespectful. It will almost certainly lead to conflict, damaged relationships or worse.

In conflict, use *your* mental space to create thinking space for *both* parties.

Conflict hurts. Few people really want to fight, especially when they see the aftermath. The mess that has to be sorted often leads to further conflict. If someone can help you find a way out of conflict or potential conflict, most people will take it. It's not a matter of ego. The person who can resolve a situation without anger or hurt is always the better for it.

By generating mental space so that protagonists can *think*, you can break into the loop of conflict at any point. What follows are ways of resolving conflict at any point during the seven stages.

1   The ideal time to prevent conflict is before it starts to develop. *Learn how to handle threats*. Don't take them personally. Most people who make the threats do so from a position of weakness. The worse they can make you feel, the stronger they will feel.

A true story

Threats come in many guises. In the age of the brain, intellectual threats are the most prevalent, and potentially the most damaging.

A group of 'friends' were playing *Trivial Pursuit* one evening. Emma hadn't wanted to play, but she joined in. They were playing in teams. The game was going fine until the host decided that there was something about Emma that he didn't like. When her team's turn came, the question was asked and the host said that he wanted Emma to answer the question. She didn't know the answer. In that instant, it turned from a game to a *threat*. Her revenge was indirect: she memorized several boxes of *Trivial Pursuit* questions. Now, when she plays, she never loses.

Emma didn't rise to the threat aggressively. That would be enough for most of us. In Emma's case, she learned from the event and made sure it never happened again. Most threats, however, are made where there *is* something to lose. If you are affected by the threat, then you have to handle step two of conflict …

2   *Fear* can arise very quickly when someone seems to be about to take something from you or do you harm. Back to the story of my friend and her boss: if she had understood her boss's reasons for threatening her, she might have spotted his agenda and manipulation more quickly. Armed with that information, she could have managed the situation differently and avoided experiencing fear.

One way of being confident in the face of threat and dealing with fear is to gather and assess information. What might be the real reason behind the obvious threat? Instead of defending yourself, smile and ask your aggressor sincerely what the problem specifically might be, then what might be an equitable solution? What will it take? What are the potential gains? What are the potential losses and how might they be avoided? They will realize that you are not going to be manipulated into a conflict and leave it at that. If, however, the situation is already emotionally charged, and if the threat did affect and perhaps frighten, know in advance how to handle step three of conflict ...

3 Interrupt *agitation*. At this stage, your emotions may have just arisen, they will still be raw, and you will be experiencing the effect of the affect: the first signs of hints of anger; offended, aggrieved, unable to muster the defence you feel in need of. You are still thinking: 'What is going on?' 'What should I do?' 'What are my options?' 'Where is the way out?' If you cannot answer these immediately, you may try to frighten your tormentor away by displaying anger, which will probably hurt you more than them. If the conflict reaches this stage, walk away, mentally rather than physically. Physically walking away may escalate the situation. Don't avoid conflict when it has reached this stage; deal with it. Stop everything and calmly take control: first of yourself, then of the situation. Say, firmly, that you don't want the situation to escalate. Perhaps get a mediator, take a break, go to lunch, think about the facts and deal with the facts. Do anything sensible and appropriate that will encourage all the parties involved to break the chain instead of turning agitation into anger. This is generally the best time to start talking of different perspectives.

Conflict occurs when people perceive the same event(s) in entirely different ways. They believe that their perspective is the right one and the only one. To some degree, they are correct; they are looking at the world from different windows of the same house. To prevent further conflict, can you generate enough mental space around the event to allow others to air their viewpoints and their views (they are not necessarily the same thing) safely and to hear and appreciate or at least acknowledge the views of others? Can you get them to stay in their rooms and close the window for a little while to think the situation through?

While this may not be easy, it is easier than dealing with anger, rage and revenge. More importantly, if you stop the conflict at this point, you are more likely to be able to sort it out entirely. Otherwise, how long will the bad feelings last? If it does escalate to anger, you have to learn how to deal with the next stage of conflict ...

4 Calming *anger*. Consider how animals behave. If you threaten an animal's space, they will make noise, bare their teeth and run at you. They may, if you are unlucky, bite you; but the intention of the display is to frighten you away. Anger in people serves a similar purpose. As well as 'emoting' you to action, it is designed to frighten others. If you watch an angry display between two people, you might notice that they invade each others' physical space, puff up their bodies to make themselves seem bigger, speak loudly, stare directly into each other eyes, sneer and spit (much like any other animal in the animal kingdom). Anger is an instinctive, unthinking display; its purpose is survival: Yours. It comes from the evolutionary choice between fight, flight or freeze.

Anger readies your physiology to deliver the energy to fight or flee; probably necessary in prehistoric days. We're smarter now. We have evolved – or are in the process of evolving – to think and relate. The only way to combat anger is to displace the emotion with thinking space and with empathy.

In angry situations, use the 'listen to your heart' exercise outlined in Chapter 3. This can calm you down almost instantly. It will help you to relate instead of retaliate. It will allow you time to think. It will also help protect you from the physiological 'fallout' of anger: increased adrenalin, high blood pressure, damage to the blood vessels that oxygenate the heart muscle, and a depressed immune system.

Remember, too, that your aggressor will be reading your body language very carefully. When you do back off, it is important to do so without seeming either patronizing or passive. Breathe slowly, pause before you say anything, speak quietly. Step back from your aggressor. Avoid staring them down. If you smile or frown at them, it may be construed as sarcastic or patronizing. Avoid looking down at their feet because this can be seen as submissive.

The aim is to give each side an exit. If none is forthcoming, the unburnt anger will lead to frustration. The consequences of frustration for your physiology can be much worse than anger partly because when you are frustrated (a stressful state) you release greater quantities of adrenalin than normal for a longer period of time. This could eventually damage you psychologically and physiologically.

Martial arts teachers say that you should disengage someone's stare by defocusing and looking either over their shoulder or between and above their eyes: through the centre of their forehead.

Take your anger to lunch

In an angry situation, it is very difficult to admit that you are wrong. That can feel like submitting to the threat of losing something. A good way of pausing the anger, calming the emotion and introducing thought and dialogue is to *take the situation to lunch,* including your protagonist. At least make the invitation.

Lunch in a public place is just that: public. It takes care of a basic need (food), and you can rely on frequent interruptions (ordering, serving, eating and so on). Invite the person with whom you are in conflict to lunch (note: that if you invite, you pay!). The purpose of the lunch is not to talk, it is to *listen.* The conflict came from somewhere. Your purpose at the lunch is to discover what the core issues are, and what can be done to resolve them or at the very least agree a process. If you can't get immediate peace, you may get agreement on beginning a peace process. You will only get the necessary information if you *ask* questions and *listen.* The important thing about listening is that you do so sincerely, and with an open mind. People will know if you are truly listening or not. If you don't, you will get nowhere. Accept that the other party has a valid point and that it makes sense to them. When you have viewed, and tried to appreciate the perspective of the other side, then they may be open to listening to *your* perspective. Between you, a compromise might be found. If you don't try, the situation is likely to worsen. You will have deprived yourself of a golden opportunity to learn ... about you and about the world.

If either your invitation or your sincere attempt to listen is declined, or if you cannot listen without emotion or you cannot otherwise find a way forward, learn how to handle the next step …

5 *Frustration* arises when you cannot find an immediate solution. You may be confused and tearful. The answer is as short as it is simple: stop looking for someone else to blame. Say to yourself, 'I am responsible' and begin to think. Only then will you be able to find ways of redressing the balance and feel better by gaining control over yourself and the situation.

6 *Redressing the balance* and emotional reset can begin when you give yourself permission to be calm. Fighting or feeling sorry for yourself will achieve little. You can either look at the information, get the situation in proportion, and work out a sensible, mature solution, or plot revenge.

7 *Revenge* infers setting out to do some degree of deliberate harm: physical, emotional or, if you can get into their wardrobe, material. Apart from the fact that the law does not take a kindly view of revenge, it can backfire and escalate to a level out of proportion to the original circumstances. If, by using your intellect with good intent, you succeed in a resolution that makes a friend of a former enemy, and both your energies blend instead of clash, the physiological sensations that you experience will be much more enjoyable than the empty sensation that can accompany the defeat of others or yourself.

It is not always obvious at a surface level that a person's behaviour always makes perfect sense to that person, in those circumstances, at that time and in that place. To properly understand, you may have to look much deeper that you are accustomed to looking.

Clean questions

Psychotherapists and counsellors earn their living by facilitating stages of self-discovery for their clients. These conversations are

mental space

momentum

intended to help them to re-organize, and to integrate new ways to think, feel and behave.

When a therapist is about to engage a client in a conversation,

an unskilled or irrelevant question might lead in a direction that results in more work than would otherwise have been required.

The client may already have been in a receptive state of mind. Their attention may be internally focused, perhaps near the point where change can begin to take place.

If the therapist asks, 'How are you feeling today?' the client might not actually be 'feeling'. They might be thinking. They might be thinking about something other than today. To answer that question, the client will have to stop thinking and try to focus on a current feeling.

Over a number of years, a counselling psychologist called David Grove put together a set of questions that he termed 'clean questions'. Some people use the term 'clean language'.

Properly trained, experienced psychotherapists will know to avoid contaminating a client's thought process.

Some of these questions can be used to defuse conflict. They are designed to question the person's *behaviour*, not the person themselves, thus avoiding making the situation more personally damaging than it is already. Since most conflict arises because people feel personally threatened, the more distance between the people and the conflict, the easier it will be to resolve the situation.

If sticks and stones can break your bones, words can really hurt you – they are *psychoactive*.

When a situation is already emotionally charged, it is important to take great care over what words you use. Angry people will re-interpret meaning to suit their own ends, even if it is illogical. These questions can help prevent that from happening:

- What would you like/do you want to have happen?

- What is it that you want (to have happen)?

- Is there anything else?

- Is there anything else about x?

- What's the relationship between x and y?

- What's the difference between x and y?

- What happened just before …?

- Then what happened?

- What happened next?

- What happened after x?

Notice that not one of these questions begins with 'why'. When you ask someone a 'why?' question, you open their minds to infinite possibilities. For instance, which would you answer more easily: Why did you do that, or what specifically caused you to do that?

Emotional reset

Conflict is emotionally destabilizing: the immune system is suppressed, adrenalin and cortisol increase (see Chapter 11), which then increases stress. It is vital to *reset* body systems after and, if you can, *during* a conflicting event. The best way is laughter.

Laughing can repair the damage anger and conflict have created.

But only if you do it sincerely! Remember, no sarcastic or politically incorrect jokes: they release the wrong hormones in you and others.

When laughter isn't the best medicine

Laughter isn't always good. Good laughter is when all parties enjoy the humour and feel unthreatened by it.

Tickling – Have you ever been tickled so hard that you can't breathe? This is closer to abuse than humour because it involves one person cornering and dominating another. It is often painful and can be offensive. This does not mean that you can't play with your child in this way: just be sensitive.

Teasing – This is usually at the expense and to the detriment of another person. It can be hurtful, embarrassing and degrading.

Laughing facts

◆ Laughing engages almost every major part of your body.

◆ When you laugh, you lose muscular control (fall over, bend over or wet yourself).

◆ Laugher exercises your diaphragm. The diaphragm separates your chest cavity and your abdomen. When you laugh, it convulses and gives your organs a much-needed massage, stimulating circulation and enhancing general wellbeing.

◆ When you laugh, your heart rate and blood pressure increase, dilating your cardiovascular system. When you stop, they decrease to below normal. Laughing ultimately lowers heart rate and blood pressure.

◆ Laughing increases oxygen intake. When we laugh, we gulp in air. Because the cardiovascular system is already dilated, the oxygen moves a lot faster to already relaxed muscles. This is one reason why you feel so good afterwards.

◆ Laughing balances the brain. During normal beta activity (see Chapter 4), the left and right sides of your brain look different under a PET (positron emission tomography) scan. When you laugh, both sides look almost identical.

- Laughing releases the body's natural opiates and pain reliever; beta-endorphins.

- When you laugh, your head and your facial muscles move. These muscles are connected to your thymus gland, which in turn is responsible for your immune system. The more you laugh, the better your immune system.

The results of this are a release of tension, extreme relaxation, bonding with fellow laughers and, very often, the end of conflict and enough mental space to work out a resolution.

Getting a giggle out

You might think it difficult to find something funny to laugh at following a conflict. A myth about laughter is that you need something to laugh at. You can laugh any time, anywhere. Either by yourself or in a group, try this exercise:

- Summarize the conflict or the reason for your anger in one sentence (for example, 'I've just lost my job', 'My tax returns are late').

- Put 'ha ha' (or ho ho, hee hee, tee hee – whichever works best for you) at the end of it, so it sounds like this: 'I've just lost my job, ha ha.'

You may have to repeat that several times and try different vowel sounds (ha ha, hee hee, tee hee, ho ho …). It won't take long for a smile to develop, then a flutter in your stomach, and eventually a good belly laugh. Tears might flow. Your emotional state will change and your body will begin to re-set itself emotionally and physically.

Honest laugher is the best medicine. In fact, one of the best ways of dealing with any conflict is to laugh, ludicrous though it may seem. It might not resolve the situation but you will feel better. When you feel better, you will be able to generate enough mental space to think about a solution.

For more information on laughing, read Annette Goodheart's book, *Laughter Therapy* (details in the resource section). It's an excellent guide to re-learning how to laugh at anything, any time, anywhere.

Saying sorry

Another guaranteed way to stop conflict is to say sorry. But only do that if you mean it. If you apologize simply to avoid a confrontation and don't sincerely mean it, resentment will build and the situation will arise again in the future.

Top ten tips on getting out of conflict unscathed

1 Don't take threats personally.

2 Take the conflict to lunch.

3 Listen with an open mind.

4 Don't go looking for conflict: there will always be someone ready to oblige.

5 Learn how to spot a manipulative bully. Be assertive.

6 Stick to the facts.

7 Slow down and think. Avoid getting loudly emotional.

8 Speak quietly and at a measured pace.

9 Aim to resolve the conflict as quickly as possible: the longer it lasts, the more difficult it will become.

10 Be sincere, honest, respectful of others' feelings, and look after yourself by making sure you reset your body – laughter really is the best. You do not need a reason to laugh – just do it!

Final thought

The more time you take to appreciate people and the good stuff, the less time you will have for conflict and the bad stuff.. Meet people for a chat and a cup of tea as often as you can, keep in touch, go to funny movies, walk in the park, and play with kids. Get them to teach you how to laugh if you have forgotten. Take time off work. Get plenty of sleep. Appreciate good food. Have fun. Relax.

Terminal seriousness is a slow way to die.

chapter eleven
memory and mental space

Memory is key to everything we do: meeting people, learning new information, planning your day. With so much practice, our memories should be excellent. Instead, many complain that not only is their memory not good enough, but that it's getting worse!

The good news is:

◆ Developing a strong, reliable memory is easy.

◆ You don't have to practise complicated mnemonics.

◆ The more relaxed you are, the better your memory will become. So roll out the yoga mat and book a massage.

A good memory is one of the best signals that you are using mental space well.

If you are stressed, frustrated, angry, fearful or bogged down with life, your memory will suffer. You may be forgetting names, appointments, conversations or what someone just told you a moment ago.

Rather than the amount of information being the major contributing factor to memory difficulties, it is our *attitude* towards it.

Memory principles

◆ Memory is not a stand-alone system; it relies on attention, perception and reasoning.

- Memory is not a system based on isolated facts. Everything you remember is interconnected to other information in memory.

- Memory retrieval relies greatly on association. The better organized you are, the more organized your memory will be and the easier it will be to recall information.

- New information is not stored separately from old information. Old knowledge helps make sense of new information and vice versa (which is why it is easier to read material you know something about).

- Memory is not only for storing information; it is designed for *use*.

- We speak about memory as if it were an object. We describe ourselves as having a good, bad or average memory, in the same way as good or bad lungs. Your memory is not a thing. It is certainly not a *single* thing. It's a series of processes taking place in your brain, *all the time*.

- Your memory can be trained. It has been said that there are no good or bad memories, just trained or untrained. Barring organic damage, and with very few exceptions, *everyone's* memory can be developed.

- One common excuse for not wanting to improve memory is 'I'm too old'. If your mind and body are healthy, age is no excuse.

- The more you use your memory, the stronger it will become. Many memory problems that people encounter as they become older are due to lack of mental exercise, lack of physical exercise, poor nutrition and excess stress.

- A basic guideline for improving memory and ability to concentrate is to focus on physical and mental health: what is good for the body is also good for the mind.

- A major factor in memory failure is stress.

- Memory includes long-term memory, short-term memory, very short-term memory, kinaesthetic memory, recall, retrieval, recognition, storage … If any one part of this process is not functioning well, your memory will be working below optimum. There is little point absorbing material without a retrieval mechanism.

◆ One final fallacy is that by memorizing too much, you will fill up your brain.

Before we discuss improving your memory by creating mental space, consider this model of your brain and how your memory works.

Remember to suit your brain

A popular theory and way of describing the brain is that it is divided into three main areas. If you hold your right hand in a fist and cover the top of your fist with your left hand, you will have an idea of what it looks like.

Reptilian brain

Your wrist represents your reptilian brain. This is the oldest part of your brain. When you were conceived, it was the first bit to develop. All animals – mammals and reptiles – have this basic brain. It keeps you alive.

Any form of physical harm or threat, intellectual, emotional, cultural, social or resource restriction alerts your reptilian brain. To function efficiently, it needs a safe environment, clear information, consideration, time, peripheral stimulation and freedom of choice. The reptilian response to stress stimuli is flight, fight or freeze.

Limbic system

Your fist represents your limbic system, also called your mammalian brain because it is common to all mammals. Amongst other things, key areas and functions are:

◆ Hippocampus: memory, storage and data retrieval.

◆ Thalamus: attention.

◆ Amygdala: emotion and pleasure.

To learn and remember, the limbic system needs:

◆ Emotion – It is easier to learn and remember what you are passionate about. Remembering someone you like or don't like is easier than remembering someone you feel neutral about.

◆ Truth – If you believe something to be true, it will be easier to remember and learn.

◆ Multisensory input – The more senses you use to absorb new information, the easier it will be to recall at a later date.

◆ Revision – Not just rote revision to memorize facts. Revise with the aim of fully understanding and integrating the new information.

◆ Demonstration – Show that you know.

To learn, the limbic system needs colour, stories, metaphor, movement, imagination, feeling and involvement.

The cortex

The hand that you used to cover the fist represents your cortex – the rational, thinking brain. It is divided into two halves connected by fibrous tissue, the corpus callosum. Generally, the left side of the brain is believed to process logic, numbers, sequential information, words and analysis. The right side processes rhythm, spatial awareness, whole pictures, imagination and dimensions. There is evidence that leads psychologists to believe that if one side of the brain is damaged or even removed (especially in young children), the other side will perform the functions that the damaged areas would have.

Which bit of the triune brain do you think has *ultimate* control?

mental space

Short-term, intermediate and long-term memory

Short-term memory holds information for just seconds. Without short-term memory every piece of information you saw, heard, smelt, touched or tasted would be instantaneously remembered and accessible. This could make gathering new information very difficult because of the interference. If you want something in your short-term memory to be available for later recall, you have to pay attention to it and take action to remember it for a longer period of time.

Intermediate memory is retained for typically two to four hours. Have you ever decided to remember something interesting then several hours later not recalled what it was? This is intermediate memory. As soon as information is no longer required, it is discarded. This is one reason why you forget people's names. You meet them once, and you remember them while you see them. After the event, you might not think about them for a while. Next time you meet them, because your visual memory is stronger than your auditory memory, you might remember where you met them and what they were wearing but you may not be able to recall their name.

Long-term memory is what people complain about most often. In reading, for instance, your short-term memory retains information long enough for you to make sense of the sentence or paragraph you are reading. Intermediate memory retains information long enough so that you can make sense of the chapter. Long-term memory helps you remember and make sense of the whole book. Long-term memory requires revision and application.

Long-term memory works with short-term and intermediate memory. As you might imagine, the three systems are interconnected. Gaps or weaknesses in one of them will prevent the whole system from working effectively.

How memory works – a simple model

There are many models that attempt to explain how the memory system works. Basically, your memory is divided into three parts:

- **Acquisition** – absorbing information via sensation, perception and interpretation.

- **Retention** – keeping it in your head.

- **Retrieval** – getting it out again.

A memory can become unavailable at any point. The trouble is, you only know it is unavailable when you try to retrieve it, e.g. you are in the company of someone whose name you have forgotten, unable to introduce them to someone whose name you have also forgotten. All is not lost; at least you *know* you have forgotten…

Some basic rules will help you improve your memory:

FOUR STEPS TO MEMORY ACQUISITION

- *Pay attention.* Most of the time you 'forget' something because you deprived yourself of the opportunity to remember it in the first place. Have you ever been introduced to someone then several seconds later you realize you have 'forgotten' their name? Chances are your attention was somewhere else – you were not present.

- *Plan.* Before you begin, think forward to when you will be likely to *use* the information. In what context will you use it? What state will you be in (calm, excited, nervous) when you want the information (exam conditions, for instance)?

- *Be interested.* Even if the event seems dull, find *something* in or about it that interests you. If you are bored, parts of your brain will not be involved, and this will make paying attention even more difficult.

◆ *Be active*. *Think* about what you are doing. Your memory does not work in isolation: the more connections you make between the new and old information, the easier it will be to understand and integrate. Understanding and integration are key to remembering.

Memory retention (storage)

Storing information in your head is one thing, but storing it in such a way that you can retrieve it later is a different matter.

Your memory thrives on *association* and *order*.

The better organized your memory, the easier it will be to retrieve information when you need it. You do not have to keep everything in your head. Be organized on paper and you will know where to find the information when you need it.

Memory needs *rehearsal* and *revision* so that it may be effectively retained and recalled. There are several ways to achieve this. Although it might not seem so at first, the *least* effective is rote rehearsal: as soon as the memory is interfered with, the information disappears. For instance, if someone gives you a telephone number then asks where you put your keys, the telephone number will fade. The loss of the keys will take your mind on a search. You will be attending to that instead of trying to store the number.

A thought experiment

Most of us learned times tables by rote. Ask a friend to say the nine times table forwards, then without allowing them time to prepare, ask them to repeat it backwards. Ask them what they had to do differently when they said it in reverse. They learned the times tables forward using the rote method, but saying it backwards uses a different memory process.

The more time you spend thinking about and understanding what you are trying to remember, the better chance you will have of remembering it.

Memory retrieval

Memories are stored in several parts of your brain. When you recall your memory of your front door, several areas of your brain will be activated. You might simultaneously:

- *See* an internal picture of your door (visual).

- *Hear* the sound of it closing (auditory).

- Recall the last time you walked through it (kinaesthetic and proprioceptive).

- Remember the *feeling* of the last time you locked yourself out (emotional).

- *Smell* the fresh coat of paint when you last painted it (olfactory).

- *Taste* the sandwich that you hurriedly ate as you rushed through the door (gustatory).

One reason we have difficulty retrieving information is that the retrieval method is inappropriate.

When we try to retrieve information, we often use only one access point. If you can recreate the *whole* experience as it was when you remembered it, it will be easier to recall more information.

Depending on how the information was originally presented, there are different types of memory retrieval. The easiest information to remember is information you can easily *recognize* and fit into an existing scheme or framework. Recognizing a face is sometimes easier than remembering the name that goes with it. When you look for information you know that you have read, you might say that you know where it is, you can see it on the page when you find the page, you recognize the text, but you cannot recall the actual piece of information itself.

Recall, is when you are given no clues at all. As opposed to recognizing a face, you have to recall the name. Most information that you forget is the information you have to recall.

Forgetting

We often become aware of our memories only when we forget something.

Memory 'failure' can happen because of disorganization, distraction or lack of awareness.

Studying the difficulties that people have when recalling information can help us understand how our memories work. Memories are often *available* (we know we have read it or seen it, and we can remember where we were when we remembered it in the first place) but the actual information is not *accessible* (just cannot quite remember it fully). This phenomenon is called 'tip of the tongue'. Most psychologists think that long-term memory is organized in categories, and that these categories are linked, much like a mind-map. One thing reminds you of the next, and so on. If these links change or become damaged in any way, then the information might become inaccessible. You might forget it entirely. 'Forget' in this sense means that you are unable to reconstruct the information.

Factors contributing to forgetting

Lack of attention (the pickpocket effect)

Problem – If you pay full attention to a task, you will not notice other things going on around you. While it might seem like a contradiction, daydreaming is one of the few activities we carry out with full attention. Next time you notice your mind wander, notice how much of your surroundings you were paying attention to. Did you notice the normal noise around you or see people moving about? Professional pickpockets know and use this. They usually work in teams of three. One is expert at absorbing your attention: he or she might bump into you quite heavily as you walk though a busy shopping precinct, then apologize with profuse charm, distracting you even further (sometimes using stage hypnosis techniques to induce an instantaneous trance). The second is expert at removing objects from your pockets or bag with minimum disturbance. The person who removes your property hands it off to a third, the runner, who takes your wallet, leaving the first two clear of any incriminating evidence.

Workaround – Improve your concentration and awareness of your surroundings. Chapter 2 can help you with this.

Interference

Problem – Interference can be retroactive or proactive. When you change your telephone number, the new one somehow latches onto your memory and replaces the old one. This is called *retroactive interference.* It comes from new information. *Proactive interference* is when old information interferes with new information. Thinking of your telephone number again, this is when you cannot remember your new one because your old number keeps coming into your mind instead.

Workaround – To work around retroactive and proactive interference, rest between different stages or pieces of work. This allows time for your mind to consolidate new information, to separate old information and to integrate new information with the framework of your existing knowledge (unless it is your telephone number).

Lack of interest or motivation

Problem – Remembering new information is almost impossible without interest or some motivation. Tiredness can contribute to this.

Even if you are interested in what you are working on, the interest will fade if you are tired.

Workaround – Find something that motivates you, no matter how small or seemingly unrelated. The task must benefit you in some way or another. Take breaks as often as you feel you need them (at least 10–15 minutes every hour to hour or so).

Insufficient links or association

Problem – If the information or job is particularly new to you, making sense of the ideas may be challenging due to your framework being in the early stage of development. If you cannot make sense of the ideas, you will find it very difficult to remember them.

Workaround – Study the glossary of terminology and any other related topics. This will help develop the mental infrastructure. Try something like making yourself familiar with legends and conventions on a road map or atlas before using it.

Insufficient revision

Problem – Memories are made of memory traces. If they are not reinforced, they will fade.

Workaround – A basic guideline is to revise seven times in ten days, or develop a very good filing system. For instance, if you want to increase your vocabulary when learning a new language, write down a number of new words every day. Each day, refer to your notebook until the older words are firmly fixed in your thinking. To remember information in the long term, *use it or lose it*.

Stress and memory

Stress destroys memory. Period.

When you are stressed, your body secretes high levels of the hormone cortisol. Cortisol affects you in a variety of ways depending on the amount released into your body. Cortisol destroys glucose, your brain's only source of food.

If you have ever witnessed or been involved in an accident or other trauma, you may have got through it. You may have appeared to other witnesses to be fully conscious. Afterwards, you may have been unable to remember anything at all, or had an incomplete memory of the incident. Extreme stress caused the release of cortisol at such a level in your bloodstream that it affected the hippocampus area of your brain and destroyed the glucose. With no food, your brain literally did not have the necessary materials to lay the long-term memory down. You saw everything. Maybe even walked around and spoke to people. But the memories were not laid down in any form that could be recalled.

It is even more complex. If your hormones go into a configuration similar to that at the time of the event, a phenomenon known as state-dependent memory can cause flashbacks as well as behavioural or mood problems. So the memory does get laid down, but not in a way that is ordinarily readily available. What might seem an inconsequential occurrence can have quite serious effects if it compounds with previous trauma. If you experience such problems after a trauma, there are several therapeutic approaches that may help.

A less extreme effect happens if, for example, you are about to give a speech, meet new people, or introduce your boss to your partner. You might feel a little fuzziness or experience other sensations. You know that you know what you should know, but you can't quite get the ideas, names or words correct. It might feel like a telephone line in a storm. The lines are there, and communication should be possible, but there's interference from somewhere.

A further scenario in which cortisol affects your brain is damaging in a slightly different way. People who live a highly stressed life have a self-induced, intravenous drip of cortisol. This cortisol destroys glucose and turns calcium into free radicals that destroy brain cells. This can cause age-related memory loss. People aged 40–50 years might feel that they're not thinking as fast and clearly as they once did. Left unchecked, these consequences can be permanent.

Providing there is no organic damage to your memory, no matter what your age or what myth you choose to believe, your memory *will* become clearer, more creative, more active and more accurate if you work at it.

Although there will be no overnight effect, constant and determined action will be rewarded. There is no magic pill for instant memory. If you choose to be, you have the natural capacity to be brilliant. It takes effort, common sense and belief in yourself.

In summary, pressure makes it difficult to remember. The first step to developing a great memory is learning how to cope with stress in situations where you need to remember.

De-stress when you need to remember

Factors that contribute to your stress levels are:

◆ The amount of information you need to remember.

◆ The time you have available.

◆ Your control over the situation.

◆ Your confidence in your ability to recall.

When you feel stressed, say 'stop' very loudly in your head, imagine everything around you freezing to a standstill, then take a mental or physical step backwards. Then:

◆ Smile, breathe deeply twice (abdominally), and stand or sit up straight.

◆ Inside your head (or out loud) laugh. A real belly laugh is a superb de-stresser.

◆ Ask those around you to slow down.

- Take your time to answer questions, and speak just a little more slowly.

- Write down information if it's appropriate.

Remember names and faces

One strategy for remembering the names and faces of those you meet is to prepare, pay attention and practise.

Prepare

Before an event, get the agenda and a guest or delegate list. Study it for names of people you have already met and perhaps know well, people you think you have met but can't remember clearly, and people you want to meet. Then prepare a strategy. Who are you going to meet first? If you want to see those you know first, walk into the room, look for those you want to speak to, and go directly to them without making eye contact with anyone else. This will prevent ambush: too many new faces as soon as you arrive. It will give you time to become familiar with the room. The best way to gain control on arrival is to arrive early and meet the people you want to meet one at a time as they arrive.

One of the golden rules of social and business networking: if you want to arrive late, become famous first.

Pay attention

The first time two people meet, they are paying more attention to visual cues than auditory information. In the first seconds while names are being exchanged, your attention is divided between building a first impression and placing the person in your social hierarchy (you are answering questions like 'Is this person useful to me?' 'Am I useful to them?' 'Am I likely to meet them again?' 'Who might they know?'). As a result, you are not paying attention to their name, and by the time you introduce yourself, you often realize you

mental space

didn't catch their name because you didn't hear it. You didn't hear it because your attention was elsewhere.

The first time you meet someone:

- Smile. Breathe slowly and abdominally. Take your time.

- Spend enough time with each person you meet to get to know something about them. As you practise, you will get faster.

- Listen carefully to the name. Say it back to make sure you are pronouncing it correctly.

- Ask the spelling if it's a difficult name or if the person mumbled.

- If the event allows, stick to first names only.

- Pay attention to the whole person, especially to the parts of them that are unlikely to change: their mannerisms, accent, posture, gestures and any unique identifying features. Hair colour, style of dress, and even eye colour (with the use of contact lenses) can change. Avoid focusing on these too much.

- Get a business card.

- Then …

Practise

Use people's names. Help them by using yours. If you forget the name, *ask for it again*. Most people will not be offended by this, but if you think they will be, then ask someone else for it.

If someone struggles to remember your name, use it in the conversation: '… and I said to myself, Tina …'

Introduce yourself when you join a group. Don't wait for someone else to do it: they might not. Say a phrase that they can associate with your name (your relation to someone they know, something you have in common with them). Smile confidently and calmly; no one wants to remember someone who frowns and scowls.

Finally, get into the habit of making introductions. Be a facilitator.

Find the pattern to a better memory

One of the greatest factors that can contribute to an improved memory is your ability to identify pattern and structure.

It is easier to remember one new piece of information and then work out how to apply it in ten different ways, than to remember ten different pieces of information.

Counting from 1 to 99 in Japanese (in 10 minutes)

English	Japanese
one	ichi
two	ni
three	san
four	shi
five	go
six	roccu
seven	shichi
eight	hachi
nine	ku
ten	ju

Before you learn how to count from one to ten in Japanese, the words mean nothing to you. The Japanese is simply a collection of sounds. To make it easier to learn, turn the sounds into something you can identify with, and turn that into an image or sensation. For example, 'ichi' sounds like 'itchy' – itchy foot. So when you want to remember the Japanese for one, remember itchy foot. 'Ni' sounds like 'knee'. 'San' sounds like 'sun. 'Shi' sounds like 'she', etc. Now, instead of memorizing random, meaningless sounds, you will be able to visualize clear images that represent the information.

When you have learned the basic structure, find the pattern.

English	Japanese
11	ju ichi
12	ju ni
13	ju san
20	ni ju
21	ni ju ichi
22	ni ju ni
23	ni ju san
30	san ju
35	san ju go

11 is 10 + 1 (ju ichi)
20 is 2 + 10 (ni ju)
21 is 2 + 10 + 1 (ni ju ichi)

When you have found the pattern, you will notice that you don't have to learn 99 different words to be able to count from 1 to 99: you only have to learn ten words and understand the structure.

Top ten tips on how to develop a great memory

1 *Be present* – listen and pay attention to what is going on around you. Most forgetting is the result of not remembering in the first place.

2 During a meeting, keep your mental space clear by listening instead of constructing your reply. Have what you want to say written down beforehand.

3 Good eating habits, plenty of exercise, a relaxed attitude and sufficient sleep all help to improve your memory. Ginkgo biloba, ginseng and lecithin may help some people.

4 The more you use what you want to remember, the easier it will be to recall later.

5 Make yourself memorable by introducing yourself slowly and clearly.

6 The more background information you know about something, the easier it will be to recall. Whether it's about a subject or a

person, ask questions about what you want to know. Have a purpose.

7   Good focus and concentration are key to good memory.

8   If possible, do one thing at a time.

9   Stick to habits. If you always put your keys in one place, you are unlikely to lose them.

10   Don't get too stressed if you happen to forget something.

Final thought

Imagine … Walking along the beach, you feel the warm sand between your toes. The warmth on your feet, sand slipping under your soles, reminds you of a holiday you took three years ago – the people you met, the fun, the beach party… Is the memory in your mind? Or is it in your toes?

12

chapter twelve
information overload

We're all deluged with information every day – especially at work: 50 emails, two trade papers and magazines, two phone calls, three pieces of post and a couple of memos – and that's before you even start.

Information has the potential to give rise to fear: 'If I don't read/understand/know this, will I be missing X, and if I do miss it, what will the consequences be?' It's not so much remembering the information that is difficult. It's the time to pay attention to it and make sense of it.

Most of the seemingly infinite information to which you have access is irrelevant to your purposes. Overloading with nonsense contributes greatly to mental block. I cannot overemphasize how important it is to identify, then ignore, irrelevant information.

The risk is much greater if you work in a large organization.

This might help: risk is defined as probability times consequence – the mathematical likelihood that something will happen multiplied by the consequences if it does happen. If you can't calculate either, then you can't calculate the risk. If you can't do that, then you shouldn't be worrying about it.

If you want your desk and your mind to remain clear, develop your ability to identify and prioritize relevance.

Sometimes you have to say no to *good* information so that you have time to work with the *best* information.

This will help prevent clutter in your mental and physical spaces.

The need to know everything

The 'need to know everything syndrome' will turn your desk into an information bottleneck and unnecessarily take up a huge proportion of your mental and physical time. Three symptoms and their cures are outlined here:

Apparent urgency – dealing with something as soon as you receive it no matter what else has to be done or how important it really is. If someone gives you a document to read and says, 'This is urgent, you must read it now', don't take their word for it. It may be urgent to them, but in your day it might come second or fifteenth. Prioritize all new work and interruptions. Stay on purpose.

Nobody does it better – excellent attitude if you want to work every weekend and most holidays. Most people are capable of doing their jobs well. Have faith in others, prioritize and *delegate*.

Generosity – When it comes to your own time, you cannot always afford to be generous. Often the people giving you something extra to deal with are trying to avoid doing what they have been tasked with. Distinguish between 'delegated' versus 'dumped on'.

Don't accept every piece of information that lands on your desk without establishing:

◆ Why you should read it (input).

◆ You are the best person to process the information (process).

◆ What you are expected to do with it (output).

Procrastination

Information that should flow may bottleneck on your desk because of *procrastination* (yours).

Procrastination may be caused by fear or lack of interest. If a task seems big or challenging, you might do other seemingly important things instead of facing the situation and dealing with it.

The cure is simple.

Determine _exactly_ what the job entails, break the job into small chunks of work, and deal with it one piece at a time.

If the cause is lack of interest, look actively for something in the task that will motivate you. If you can find nothing that interests you and your desk is always full of paperwork that you can't be bothered with, you might consider re-negotiating your job description or finding a different job.

A successful and proven method of managing non-fiction material is the five-step reading strategy outlined in the introductory chapter. If you need to refresh your memory, go back to Chapter 1 and re-read it. In addition to the five-step strategy, there are a number of other techniques you can use to help minimize the unwanted information you are presented with.

Prioritize information

The more effectively you prioritize your reading, the faster you will process it. You will be surprised at how much you can achieve when you enlist the help of others and share information. When unread material piles so high that you feel you can't do anything about it, you will feel exhausted before you approach your desk, commonly known as 'paper fatigue'.

To prioritize effectively:

◆ Gather all your backlogged reading or paperwork.

◆ Sort it into groups:
- _Urgent_ – if you don't read/deal with this, something, somewhere will go drastically wrong … soon. Or, if you do you will make something good even better.
- _Important_ – if you don't deal with/read this now, the world won't collapse, but if you leave it too long, it might.

- *Useful* – information that would be good to know but is not urgent.
- *Nice to know* – information that is good to have access to, but if you never read it, it wouldn't matter. This might include magazine and newspaper articles you thought looked interesting.
- *Bin* – bin!

◆ Start with the urgent stack. Sort it into *pay-off* or *rip-off*. Will the document make you money (give you value) or cost you money if you do not deal with it? If any documents in the urgent pile don't fit either, they may not be so urgent. Are they urgent because someone else said so? What will be your commitment and contribution to the project?

◆ Quickly assess the length of time it will take to read each document. Plan the reading into your day based on when you will need the information. If you read something that you will not use for several weeks, you will most likely have to re-read it at that time. Date it and read it when it is necessary (sometimes procrastination is the right thing to do).

If you consistently receive documents that you don't need, it can be annoying and time wasting. Receiving as little junk mail as possible will help make daily prioritization much easier.

Reduce your junk mail intake

◆ Collect all reports, journals, documents, emails and memos not related directly to your job that arrive on your desk during a typical month.

◆ Establish any patterns: Does the same person or office consistently send irrelevant material? Is it vital to your job? Have you any interest in the subject matter? Do they arrive regularly without you asking for them? Have you requested them? If so, for what specific purpose?

◆ When you have established which documents are beneficial to you, briefly study each one. Is it written such that you can gather information without reading the whole document? How long would it take to read the summaries and conclusions? Would it be sufficient? If you don't need to read the whole document, does the writer know? If you only receive what you need, you could both save time.

◆ Determine the actions required to take forward the issues arising from the documents. If most of the reports and memos are for information only, and they don't place any actions on you, then their urgency and their importance will diminish.

◆ Could you get the information by speaking briefly to someone, perhaps under the guise of socializing for a few minutes?

◆ Is the information still valid by the time you receive it? Or is it old news?

◆ If you are not clear that you *have* to read something, put it aside as a test. If someone asks you to act on it, you may have to pay attention to it in the future.

◆ When you have categorized the material, prioritize it as discussed earlier. If you don't need the reports or memos, ask to be excluded from the mailing list.

Top ten tips on avoiding information overload

1 Have your purpose clearly in mind when you review any information.

2 Set a time limit for how long you will spend on dealing with information.

3 When dealing with mail, make the bin the preferred option.

4 Prioritize incoming information as quickly as possible.

5 Keep your desk clear of *everything* except your current project.

6 Do unto others … don't send junk mail to other people.

7 Don't just store information: use it.

8 If your filing system does not work for you by helping you find information efficiently, change it. Is it your system? Does it have to be like anybody else's?

9 Don't assume that others either know or want to know everything you know or do.

10 Good questions attract good information. Think of the kind of answers you want when you ask questions.

Final thought

A very successful businessman I know has a tough attitude towards mail, reports and memos. He follows the advice of the World War II pilot Douglas Bader. All mail goes straight in the bin. His belief is that if something is important enough, someone will contact him personally. Perhaps it's too much of a high-risk strategy, but it highlights that we should be selective about what we invest our time in reading.

mental space

momentum

chapter thirteen
problem solving and creativity: think like a genius

How 'the greats' did it

What if geniuses are just ordinary people who stumble on a knack or way of thinking that enables them to think and learn more effectively and creatively than others?

People like Newton or Archimedes didn't simply sit under trees or in baths until they became enlightened. They used some very powerful and practical tools to create order out of their thoughts and to find answers to problems that few people even thought existed, let alone attempted to solve.

The tools used by geniuses are as applicable to you as they are to the great thinkers.

When faced with a challenging problem, these techniques will help clear your head, generate more than one workable solution to a given problem, think creatively (productively instead of *re*productively) and give you a clear methodology that will simplify problem solving.

Some factors common to the world's great thinkers:

◆ Ideas are generated in *pictures* and *images* rather than words. Einstein and Leonardo da Vinci drew diagrams instead of writing words and sentences.

◆ Their thinking is *unrestrained:* nothing is rejected until it has been investigated fully.

◆ Thoughts are *things*.

- Ideas are explored using *association*.

- They look at ideas from different *perspectives*.

- They are *prolific*.

- They *record* everything.

- They fuel their imaginations with *knowledge*.

- Their thinking is *focused*.

- They are *passionate* and *determined* about discovery as a discipline.

- Instead of seeing *mistakes* and *unexpected results* as failures, they welcome them as opportunities to learn how *not* to do it.

- They see *potential* in everything.

- They never give up.

Basic brain facts (until we know better)

The phenomenal thing about studying the human mind is that we will never really know how it works.

Since you have to *use* your brain to think about your brain, it follows that whatever you have done with your brain so far – thinking, creating, imagining – is the very least you are capable of.

In case there is any doubt about your ability to do some amazing thinking, here are a few facts about your hardware (your brain). This information serves only to remind us that we are owners of an amazing tool that we will probably never fully utilize.

- You have a trillion (give or take) brain cells.

- 100 billion (give or take even more) are nerve cells.

- Each of the 100 billion nerve cells can grow up to 20,000–30,000 branches.

- Every idea you have, every new thought you generate, everything you see, hear, smell, touch, taste and learn makes these branches grow.

- The growth of new cells far outweighs the damage to existing cells thoughout your life.

- The more you use your brain – thinking, learning, reading, daydreaming – the stronger your mind becomes.

Paraphrasing Einstein: the level of thinking that gets you into a mess will not get you out of it.

Thinking differently gives insight into problems. The closer you are to a problem, the less able you might be to solve it. Giving yourself mental space allows you to be more creative and to uncover solutions more readily.

Few things are more personal and subjective than the way you think. Great thinkers have the *will* to try something new. They are happy to get it wrong the first time around. They have the *belief* that they are capable of thinking originally and creatively, the *desire* to explore their limits, and the *energy* to think.

'I'm thinking all the time,' you might say. 'In fact, I'm thinking so much it's difficult to empty my head!' Take a little time to think about what occupies your mind most of the day. Do you think about yesterdays meeting? Today's agenda? Last night's dinner? Tonight's dinner? An argument you had last week? An argument you would like to have today so that you have the opportunity to say what you wanted to say last week? Do you think about what you have done? Do you think about what you wish you would do? Or do you have *new* and *original* thoughts? In answer to a question about how she views her projects, actress and singer Kylie Minogue said that she never looks back. She finishes the current piece of work and then moves forward.

Original thinking happens when you look at ideas from a number of different perspectives.

When you combine concepts in novel ways, it allows you to perceive the world differently. This type of thinking helps you to learn and think fast and effectively: to apply that thinking and new information in different contexts. It will help you remember what you learn, and recall it when needed. It will also help you be more creative, solve complex problems and communicate more effectively.

Darwin lives: natural selection favours thinkers

'Survival of the fittest' infers the ability to *learn* and, more importantly, to *adapt*. To survive in a complex environment, a species either adapts and thrives, or become extinct. That depends on the combined activities of individuals in that species. The characteristics of an organism are important in determining whether it survives as a species. Take a mouse for instance: you might think that a mouse with long legs would have a better chance of surviving than one with short legs – long legs mean it can run faster, escape danger and live another day to reproduce. So, why don't we have supersonic, high-speed, long-legged mice? Long legs have disadvantages as well as advantages. A mouse with very strong, long legs would need more food to deliver the energy to move fast. The muscle bulk required for strength and speed means that it will be bigger than shorter-legged counterparts, but there are fewer places that it can use to hide from its enemies. Through evolution, the mouse has developed an *optimal* length and strength of leg to ensure that it can move efficiently while remaining small enough to hide in places predators cannot reach. While some individual mice might develop extraordinarily long legs, the mouse species in general does not, because it would not be good for the survival of the species as a whole.

Now consider humans and genius: why is it that only a small percentage of the population are geniuses? What would be the advantages or disadvantages if the population as a whole were to perform to their highest physical, emotional, psychological and intellectual capacities? What would the world be like if everyone used and developed these talents?

Unlike mice, we are at the top of the food chain. Except for a very small number of other humans from whom we have to run or hide, we have no predators in our cities.

There is no need or reason to limit our development.

Yet, despite the potential we are all born with, very few people become the best they can be. I suggest that it's because we are not taught how.

If it is true that geniuses are ordinary people who have stumbled on a knack or way of thinking that enables them to learn more effectively and think more creatively than others, then could it be that *everyone* has the ability to be a Mozart, an Einstein or a Leonardo. They were just as baffled as the rest of us as to how they managed to generate such astonishing ideas, discoveries and inventions? Most displayed their genius at such a young age that it was quite simply the way they thought and behaved.

The rest of this chapter explores some of the tools of the great thinkers in history. Think about how you might use each of these techniques to enhance your own thinking skills. Shift from *surviving* to being *supersonic*.

The trick is insight

When you start to think about learning something new, you might have some knowledge on the subject or you may know very little or nothing at all about it.

The *resources* – books, cassettes, videos, lectures, journals, papers or demonstration – are rarely presented such that the first thing you need to know about the subject is at the beginning, and the rest of the information structured so that it makes sense as you learn.

Many people spend the first few hours, months or even years in confusion when starting to learn or think about new information because the concepts that will help them understand the subject and how the ideas come together are either not laid out clearly at the beginning or are missing entirely.

To think clearly and originally, it may help to be able to organize information in a way that will enable you to understand the subject from the beginning. Not to say that you should expect to understand everything immediately, rather that you will be able to make sense of it. In making sense, it will be easier to learn, remember, recall and integrate with other related ideas.

The trick is gaining *insight* and reaching the 'Aha!' stage as quickly as possible. Sometimes it's as simple as having the definitions of certain key terms.

There are three processes involved in successfully gaining insight at an early stage:

1 **Encoding:** *sorting* out the *relevant* information from the *irrelevant* quickly.

2 **Combining:** *combining* the relevant information in a *meaningful* way.

3 **Comparison:** *comparing* old information with new.

The following tools are designed to help you to achieve insight as early in your thinking as possible.

Tools for creating mental space and generating genius thinking

Mapping

Before exploring these techniques, it is worth talking about information mapping. Mind-mapping was formalized and labelled by Buzan in the 1970s. Great thinkers have used similar techniques for centuries. Like other geniuses, Leonardo da Vinci, Albert Einstein and Thomas Edison represented their ideas through diagrams and 'maps'. A completed map may look something like this:

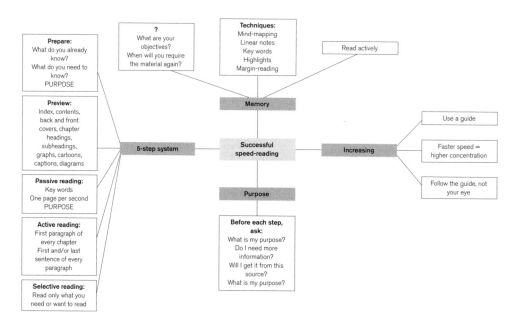

- Pictures instead of words.

- Links between related ideas.

- The main concepts are in the middle, gradually becoming more detailed towards the end of the braches.

- Single words or ideas per line.

- Colour.

Some of the benefits of information mapping include:

- Getting an impression of the bigger picture.

- Not limited to linear thinking, as when you write an idea in words, sentences and paragraphs.

- Your mind thinks faster in pictures than it does in words.

- Links between previously unrelated ideas are made quickly and more easily.

- Easier to mentally represent a picture than linear text.

Taking mind-mapping a step further

Some people who use mind-maps generate the information then immediately get practical with it. However, adding two steps in-between *generating* the content of the mind-map and *using* the information makes it even more creative and useable:

- Do the *generative* stage as you would normally: write down everything that comes into your head – free associate – don't edit out anything just yet. Write down one word or idea per line.

- *Change perspective*: link the unlinkable ideas, write the opposite of what you wrote originally, exaggerate the idea (instead of saying X *sometimes* happens, say that it *always* happens or vice versa), change the gender, race, age, political or religious bias of people on the map.

- *Stand in someone else's shoes*: if you are in a new job, mentally put yourself in your boss's, customer's, bank manager's or partner's shoes and re-draw the map. What are the differences between the first and the second maps? Now, imagine you were the best in the world at whatever is the main activity of the project, and re-draw the map once more. Open your mind. Write down what comes to your awareness, even if it seems to make no sense at all.

- Finally, *formalize your thinking*: focus on your outcome. Review the maps you drew at each of the above stages. Select and develop those ideas that you *know* will contribute most to your project.

System thinking

Edison didn't invent just a light bulb; he invented an entire system on which a multitude of light bulbs could function. Thinking in terms of a system will allow you to see the whole picture with all its interconnected and interacting components. Integrating the entire system will give a deeper insight and accelerates creative thinking.

Applying system thinking – making sense of a system

◆ Write down what you perceive the problem to be e.g. general performance of your team is not up to standard).

◆ Consider the symptoms or conditions that led you to that view (e.g. late arrival, low motivation, agitated behaviour between colleagues, missing deadlines).

◆ List each symptom and write down, against each, *all* their possible causes. Be as unbiased as possible (e.g. possible causes for missing deadlines – working late hours, unclear job descriptions, unclear management decisions, unreasonable timescales, etc.).

◆ Now consider each cause; assess the *extent* to which each contributes to the situation (e.g. do people work late hours? Are timescales unreasonable? Is communication between staff and management clear?). It is often worthwhile using an external mediator to remove bias.

◆ When you have determined some definite causes, work on what can be done to resolve the issue and prevent recurrence.

One reason this technique works is that instead of accusing your team of poor performance and setting the scene for blame and subsequent denial, you are asking questions that give people the opportunity to examine their performance without feeling singled out or threatened. Asking questions might establish that poor performance is due to people feeling obliged to work late most nights, and becoming exhausted. Unlike general poor performance, this is clearly defined. There is now an opportunity to take remedial action.

Many commentators assert that more than 90 per cent of work performance problems are due to the inadequacies of the system in which people work and are therefore outside the influence of the individual worker, unless, of course, he or she is invited to contribute.

It's important to carry out this exercise with *all* the people involved. It's also important to make it a safe, open forum so that people feel free to contribute without thinking that one wrong answer could generate a P45/pink slip.

Lily pond

T.S. Elliot used a system in which he started with one idea or theme, surrounded that theme with a number of subthemes, then repeated that with each subtheme. The end result looked to him like a pond covered in lilies with connecting stems. This technique allows you to explore the theme gradually and in great detail, without losing ideas or creating confusion.

BUILDING THE LILY POND

◆ Build a 9x9 grid. That will give you 81 squares.

◆ Because of the odd number, you will have a central square. State the problem simply and clearly in that square.

◆ Around the problem, write eight possible solutions (A to H).

◆ Now, write each solution in each 'lily' surrounding the centre one.

◆ Generate ideas around each of these solutions.

A1	A2	A3	B1	B2	B3	C1	C2	C3
A8	Solution A	A4	B8	Solution B	B4	C8	Solution C	C4
A7	A6	A5	B7	B6	B5	C7	C6	C5
H1	H2	H3	Solution A	Solution B	Solution C	D1	D2	D3
H8	Solution H	H4	Solution H	Problem	Solution D	D8	Solution D	D4
H7	H6	H5	Solution G	Solution F	Solution E	D7	D6	D5
G1	G2	G3	F1	F2	F3	E1	E2	E3
G8	Solution G	G4	F8	Solution F	F4	E8	Solution E	E4
G7	G6	G5	F7	F6	F5	E7	E6	E5

Five-level pyramid thinking strategy

The pyramid thinking strategy is easy to apply to any subject or problem.

Successful thinking is not based so much on what you think – rather, it is the way you think that makes the difference.

A difficulty that people often have when they are tackling a complex problem is that they study it linearly (beginning to end, as the information was presented to them). This makes integrating new ideas and considering the problem from different angles difficult.

This strategy encourages you to reorder ideas and new information. Summarize your problem or subject and consider it in light of the following questions.

Pyramid level 1
What do you already know?
What do you need to know?
What are your sources?
What are further sources?
Who do you know that knows more than you on this topic?

Pyramid level 2
Determine as many of the key concepts on the *whole* subject as you can.
Gather main definitions, ideas and key pieces of information for each concept.

Pyramid level 3
Link the concepts together and add further details by using the five-step reading system for effective research and study.

Pyramid level 4
Ask yourself the following questions about each link:
Why does the link exist?
What is the relationship between the links?
What impact does the link have on the subject as a whole?
How and with what else are the concepts linked?
If I were to stretch my imagination, how could these ideas be linked?

Pyramid level 5
Add to each link:
What, why, who, when, where, how, details …
Compare each link with others and with previous knowledge.
Return to key concepts determined in level 1.

Top ten tips on solving problems, creativity and thinking like a genius

1 Be brave and adventurous in your thinking.

2 Think beyond what you know.

3 The bigger the problem looks, the greater the need to ensure that it is solved by rational *thinking* rather than *emoting* (although it is good to become excited).

4 Communicate with other minds. Talk. Listen. Ask. Listen again. Get perspectives from people around you.

5 Never assume the first answer is the right one.

6 Develop a positive attitude towards problems. The more you deal with them, the better you will get.

7 Never procrastinate actions, but never make decisions in haste. Whenever you identify a problem, deal with it.

8 Remember: your problem is probably not the greatest problem on earth, neither is it likely to be life threatening. Keep things in perspective.

9 Never let others bully you into either action or inaction. If it's *your* problem, *you* solve it. Listen to opinions, but keep your own counsel, unless of course they really do have a better idea.

10 Sleep on it. If you can't, just get on with fixing it. However, don't passively hope that something will happen by itself or that the problem will go away by itself.

Final thought

My dad has a great attitude towards problems. As kids, my two sisters and I went to him with our problems. Rubbing his hands together, he would grin and say, 'Problems, problems, I *love* problems!' Then he would start us off working on our *own* solutions. Kids are smart, let them sort out their own issues; support them with love and encouragement. If necessary, give them just enough clues that will let them experience a healthy struggle.

chapter fourteen
perfect (and when good is good enough)

mental space

momentum

We all have our own definition of 'perfect'. You could work so that everything is perfect for you. Ten people could look at your 'perfect' finished product, and each might find at least one thing they didn't like.

Aiming for perfection makes sense if, and only if, no one else will have an interest in the outcome.

If others are going to have input, then a *compromise* is as good as you will get. For perfectionists, this may be difficult.

There are two main categories of perfectionist

◆ *Time perfectionists* – people who will do *whatever* it takes to meet a deadline. Quality be damned, meet the deadline. This type of perfectionist will find shortcuts to ensure they meet deadlines, often with time to spare. They are so focused on completion that they miss opportunities and alternatives. They don't take time out to explore options. Working with time-perfect people can be difficult when they are rushing and creating their own mini deadlines throughout the project instead of letting the project flow.

◆ *Quality perfectionists* – people who will sacrifice time for quality. Their motto is, 'If you want it right, you'll have to wait.' The job is not complete until every aspect is checked, double-checked and confirmed. The finished product might be perfect in their eyes, but flawed as far as others are concerned (especially if being on time was one of the pre-conditions). This type of perfectionism can be a smoke screen for lack of confidence. If you can't submit work because it's not finished / perfect, is it a lack of confidence, fear of disapproval, fear of failure or fear of success that stops you? Those who suffer from quality perfectionism don't believe that anyone can do the job as well as they can, and as a result do much more work than necessary.

Perfectionists don't believe that there is anything wrong with the way they work, because they are … perfect. If you recognize yourself at least in part in one of these categories, and admit that perhaps the way you work is not perfect, then there is hope for you.

Solutions

If you are time perfect:

◆ When someone asks, 'How long will it take?' pause, take a deep breath, think about what you would normally say, then double or treble it. If you finish early, then great, but *be realistic,* and give yourself the time to think about quality as well.

◆ Learn to feel comfortable about *extended deadlines.* As discussed in Chapter 7, *some* deadlines are flexible. There may be time to spare. If you do it too often you may lose credibility. Before you extend a deadline, consider what happens to your work when you pass it on. If you extend the delivery date very far beyond the agreed date, it might cause difficulty and inconvenience for those who have to have input in your output.

◆ If you work in a team on a project and time is a critical factor, it is important to be very clear and honest with them about the deadlines and what needs to be achieved. Non-time-perfect people will be frustrated if they are given untrue deadlines. If there are ten weeks to complete a project and the time-perfect team leader tells the team that there are in fact only eight weeks, the leader is putting the team in a position of completing in less than eight weeks what would normally take ten weeks. This will undoubtedly affect the team's performance, stress levels and quality of work. If the team discovers that they did in fact have ten weeks, they will lose faith in the leader. He or she will find it difficult to be taken seriously in the future. Be honest, and be realistic. People are capable of managing their own time; you don't have to do it for them.

At the start of a project, be honest with the team. Tell them exactly how much time they have to complete the project, and create a plan highlighting key dates when parts of the project have to be completed. Make sure everyone has input into the plan and is aware of it.

If you are quality perfect:

◆ It is important that you consider more than your own ideas of a project outcome. Perfect for one person does not mean perfect for another. Whether performance, writing, product design or construction, always have the *audience* in mind. Whose opinion really counts? Thousands of small, medium and large businesses fail every year because at some time they build their business around what *they* think is right rather than what the customer wants. Think of the end user. Think of the audience.

◆ When balancing the possible and the perfect, it is important to have a good sense of when good is good enough. Things can always be better. Improvement can only happen if there is something to improve on. If you don't close a project and put it out into the world, you will never find out what your market would like to improve in it. Needs change, and what was once perfect becomes either inadequate or unwanted.

Achieving balance

'Fit for purpose' should be the new motto of recovering perfectionists. Make it perfect to the degree of being fit for purpose. This means that your work should:

◆ Perform the job required.

- Suit the needs of end users and audiences.

- Be within time and budget and to specification.

- Be completed with minimum stress and frustration.

- Be open to continuous improvement. Perfectionists are not keen to allow others to suggest improvements – if it's perfect there is no need for improvement, right?

Top ten tips on being a balanced perfectionist

1 Relax. Stop being so uptight.

2 Acknowledge that others are capable of doing a good job.

3 Get the facts and establish what is required rather than imposing your arbitrary decision on what is required.

4 Keep the end user in mind.

5 Have confidence in your work.

6 Be open to criticism, adjustments and improvements to your work.

7 Respect the input of others.

8 Have an open mind with respect to new ideas and alternatives.

9 Don't feel obliged to do everything yourself. Avoid re-work just because it's not exactly what you would do. If the results are the same, then let it be.

10 Sometimes good is better than perfect.

Final thought

There are times when perfection is not just a necessity, it is a top priority, e.g. the maths for a moon landing, the process in a surgical procedure. In most other cases, perfectionism can be a hindrance. Striving for perfection first time round prevents you from trying options or experimenting. Have the wisdom to decide when to be perfect, good, excellent, or not to care at all. The skill is knowing when perfection is the enemy of excellence.

mental space

15

chapter fifteen
relationships and mental space

Some years ago, I attended a workshop on presentation skills. To assess the delegates, the facilitator asked each of us to give a two-minute speech entitled 'Who am I?' The 18 people at the workshop delivered similar content, almost word for word. They defined themselves in terms of their relationships: 'I am Sue/Joe, married, a mother/father of 2.4 children, I have three sisters and one brother …'

Often, we think that we *are* our relationships. Ever spent more than a few days alone? Found that you don't know what to do with yourself?

True. We all need people. People need us in return. Regardless of how many relationship roles we play, we are unique individuals. Relationships of all kinds occupy a huge amount of mental space, and it's worth looking at how much, and whether they occupy too much and are therefore unhealthy.

Blood thicker than water

Most cultures teach that blood is thicker than water. Unlike friendships, you didn't choose your family. Yet, the bonds within families are unique among relationships. Within families, bad behaviour is forgiven more readily than anywhere else.

If friends behaved as badly as some family members, the friendship would likely dissolve.

Yet with families, there is a seemingly indestructible tie. This is both good and bad. Your family may be the most reliable, loving, dependable people you will ever know. They can equally be the cause of extreme emotional or physical pain.

When relationships are damaging, it is important not to be blinded by beliefs and emotions.

Whether in families or other social relationships, it is important to recognize and distinguish between love, care, devotion and manipulation, abuse, obsession. Some of the greatest harm is done in the name of family love. Just because the bond is strong, no one has the right to abuse the trust of another. If your family are doing you harm, emotionally, physically or psychologically, deal with it. If you have to, get help.

We're in relationships only because we need to be

Think about a partner, whether current or previous. What attracted you to that person? What did that person give you? What did that person have that you needed? The key word is 'need'.

Most partnership-type relationships exist because two people get something they need from each other.

If either partner stops meeting the needs of the other, a tension arises in the relationship. Does it begin to fail? Do the two commit to coming to a compromise? Does one or other partner always seem to 'win'? Is the relationship based on win/win or win/lose? Think of relationships of yours that failed. Do you know specifically why they did not succeed? What did you need that your partner could not provide or vice versa?

People want to be together when needs are met.

Harsh?

True!

Expectations

Is a father good if he works all hours in a job that does not fulfil him to provide for his family? Is a mother good if she devotes her life to provide for her children? Are children good provided they live up to parental expectations? Good friends behave in socially expected ways.

If you live by expectations alone, you will cease to live your own life and become a social chameleon.

Child-like with parents, parental with your children, employee-like at work. What about you? Where are you in all of this?

We all have legal, social and moral obligations to each other. These are not the same as what your family might expect you to do. For example, if you have children, you are obliged to provide for them. Providing a safe and loving environment in which they can grow and develop. You do not have to sacrifice your dreams because society expects you to behave in a certain 'parental' way. Some of the best educated, socially balanced, and happy children have parents who live their dreams. Some of the most damaged children have parents who decide not to pursue their dreams. The consequences of doing what is expected instead of fulfilling your dreams will eventually adversely affect the children you are trying to protect.

Some years ago, I led a television discussion on success and achievement. A woman in the audience said her family didn't support her in pursuing her dream. She asked what she should do. Doing what she wanted to do regardless of family considerations would have meant that ultimately she would lose them. However, not fulfilling her ambition would mean that they would lose her. In a situation like this, it is vital to maintain dialogue, compromise, compassion and love.

People will not support ideas if they do not understand them fully or if they feel threatened by them. If a mother wants to return to work, her family might object. They may fear that some of their needs might not be met. If you want your dream to succeed, it is important to take the time to gradually win approval and acceptance of those who will be affected by your decisions.

If those close to you will not acknowledge your dreams, make a sincere attempt to see the situation from their point of view. What are their reasons? What might they be afraid of losing? What will change in their lives if you change yours?

Your primary responsibility is to yourself. If you are unhappy and unfulfilled, you will not give your best to those around you.

'Selfish' behaviour

Many of those who 'sacrifice' their lives for others resent it. They believe that others should be as unhappy as they are. They want to be martyrs. There is no such thing as someone who sacrifices their entire life to others without regard for their own needs or expecting anything in return. Think of some of the great humanitarians. They had a purpose. They acted because of their beliefs. They got something in return for their actions. It may not be obvious, but it makes sense to them.

Imposing your values and expectations onto others and expecting them to oblige is selfish behaviour.

Creating space in relationships

◆ Get time alone every day. If you can't enjoy your own company, you can't expect others to.

◆ Don't insist on knowing what everyone is doing all the time. Respect their physical, mental and emotional space.

◆ Don't assume you know the needs and thoughts of those around you.

- Have interests unique to you. Don't intrude on the unique interests of others. Hobbies are often developed as a means of creating personal space. People choose activities that they are very interested in and are unlikely to interest those close to them. A typical stereotype: he plays golf, she plays bingo.

- Learn to enjoy silence. Nothing takes up mental space faster than someone constantly filling it with pointless chatter.

- Take time to think about your own opinions and ideas. Avoid being caught in the 'smart suit trap' (agreeing with anyone who looks like they might know more than you – they often don't).

- Enjoy being challenged. The more ideas you have that cause people to ask questions and debate, the stronger and more independent your thinking will become. Have courage to speak your mind, defend your ideas, and, more importantly, adapt them in the light of new evidence.

- Don't be too bothered by the opinions others have of you. Their expectations and standards are usually based on what they expect of themselves.

Communication and relationships

Try this out with five other people.

- Everyone get a sheet of paper and a pen.

- On the left-hand side, list these categories: money, success, love, sex, work and play, leaving a few lines between each.

- Then write down ten words that you associate with each category.

- Compare the lists.

How many commonalities are there? Don't be surprised if there are none. We might all have a common understanding of the general meaning of the words we use but we all have our own definitions.

When a loving relationship breaks down, it might be because two people are talking about love, but their definitions of love are different.

In the study of neurolinguistic programming (NLP) you would be taught the visual, auditory, kinaesthetic theory of communication: each of us has a dominant sense. Visual people will use 'visual words': 'I see, it's clear to me now, show me.' Kinaesthetic people will use 'feeling words': 'Gut feel, get a good vibration.' Auditory people will use 'sound words': 'I hear you, that sounds good.' Olfactory and gustatory people similarly use words associated with smell and taste. The theory is that if a visual person uses 'visual words' to speak to an auditory person, communication may fail because the auditory person cannot relate to visual words. Whether or not that theory is true, there is more to communication.

Communication consists not only of what people say; they also have gestures, stances, tics and a number of sounds such as sighs, sniffs, coughs and more. Not to mention beliefs, taboos, values and a lifetime of fears, uncertainties, dreams and unconscious thoughts. When communication breaks down, it is not surprising that it is difficult to explain why.

If you want to avoid a breakdown of communication:

Never assume that you know what people are thinking or are going to say. Not only is it rude, you will almost certainly be wrong.

Never finish someone's sentences for them, especially if you hardly know them.

Instead, ask questions. Listen to the answers.

mental space

Top nine tips on better relationships

1 Give due consideration to others and do no harm.

2 Do whatever it takes to feel good about yourself.

3 People are more complicated than you can imagine. Never assume you can accurately 'read' them.

4 Be aware of bullying and manipulative relationships.

5 Have the courage of your opinions and convictions.

6 Don't be a doormat. Don't treat others like one.

7 Decide how much time you would like to spend on your own. Plan your activities so that you get it. Learn to enjoy quiet, peace and solitary thinking.

8 Don't assume people can read *your* mind – speak up.

9 Don't judge people by your standards, theirs might be higher.

Bette Middler, singer and actress, is reported to have said, 'I have my standards. They may be low, but I have them.'

Final thought

Look beyond differences in culture, belief, politics, colour, religion or gender. *All* humanity has one thing in common: we all want to be appreciated.

chapter sixteen
resources for continued development

mental space

\ momentum

These are just a few of the books and resources available to you to continue your development. In some cases, the entire book is brilliant; others will have gems hidden in them that are worth looking for. Look for and gather new information so that you have enough to make up your *own mind*.

www.tinakonstant.com: Information on the authors of *Mental Space*.
www.yourmomentum.com: Pearson website featuring the momentum books and pages from *Mental Space* that you can download.
www.business-minds.com: A wealth of career and business information and advice.
www.teehee.com: Annette Goodheart's laughter website.
www.heartmath.org: For more information on the Heartmath Institute and Freeze-Frame.

Beaver, D. (1994) *Lazy Learning*. Dorset, UK: Element.
Berger, D. (2000) *The Motely Fool UK Investment Guide*. London: Boxtree.
Berry, C. (1994) *Your Voice and How to Use it Successfully*. London: Virgin Books.
Cava, R. (1999) *Dealing with Difficult People*. London: Piatkus.
Cialdini, R. (2000) *Influence: Practice and Science*. Boston: Addison-Wesley Education.
Conradi and Hall (2001) *That Presentation Sensation*. London: Financial Times Prentice Hall.
Decker, B. (1989) *How to Communicate Effectively*. London: Kogan Page.
Denny, R. (1994) *Speak for Yourself*. London: Kogan Page.
DePorter, B. and Hernacki, M. (1995) *Quantum Learning*. London: Piatkus.

Dilts, R.B. (1994) *Effective Presentation Skills*. Capitola: Meta Publications.

Dryden, G. and Jeanette, V. (1994) *The Learning Revolution*. Aylesbury, UK: Accelerated Learning.

Dudley, G.A. (1986) *Double your Learning Power*. London: Thorsons.

Fenn, C. (1997) *Forget the Fear of Food*. Forward Press.

Fenn, C. (1997) *The Energy Advantage*. London: Thorsons.

Fisher, R. (1992) *Getting Past No*. London: Random House.

Forsyth, P. (1995) *Making Successful Presentations*. London: Sheldon.

Furst, B. (1962) *The Practical Way to a Better Memory*. London: R&W Heap.

Grant, T. and Greene, J. (2001) *Coach Yourself*. London: Momentum.

Grove, D. (1989) *Resolving Traumatic Memories: Metaphors and Symbols in Psychotherapy*. New York: Irvington Publishers.

Hermann, D., Raybeck, D. and Gutman, D. (1996) *Improving Student Memory*. Gottingen: Hogrefe and Huber.

Hooper, J. and Teresi, D. (1992) *The Three Pound Universe*. New York: Tarcher Putnam.

Hunt, D.T. (1993) *Learning to Learn*. Oregan: Elan.

Jay, (2001) *Fast Thinking Managers Manual*. London: Financial Times Prentice Hall.

Jay, (2001) *Fast Thinking Presentation*. London: Financial Times Prentice Hall.

Khalsa, D.S. (1997) *Brain Longevity*. London: Century.

Kiyosaki, R.T. (1998) *Rich Dad, Poor Dad*. London: Warner Business Books.

Kiyosaki, R.T. (2001) *Rich Dad, Poor Dad's Guide to Investing*. London: Warner Business Books.

Konstant, T. (2000) *Speed-reading in a Week*. London: Hodder and Stoughton.

Konstant, T. (2000) *Teach Yourself Speed-reading*. London: Hodder and Stoughton.

Lorayne, H. and Lucas, J. (1974) *The Memory Book*. Dorset, UK: Element.

Luria, A.R. (1968) *The Mind of a Mnemonist*. New York: Harvard.

Markham, U. (1993) *Memory Power*. London: Vermillion.

McConnell, C. (2001) *Change Activist*. London: Momentum.

Michalko, M. (2001) *Cracking Creativity: The Secrets of Creative Genius*. Berkeley: Ten Speed Press.

Mirsky, N. (1994) *The Unforgettable Memory Book*. London: BBC.

Morrison, M. (2001) *Clear Speech*. London: A&C Black.

O'Connor, J. and Seymour, J. (1994) *Training with NLP*. Kent, UK: HarperCollins.

Ostrander, S. and Schroeder, L. (1992) *Cosmic Memory*. New York: Simon and Schuster.

Ostrander, S. and Schroeder, L. (1994) *Superlearning 2000*. London: Souvenir Press.

Rose, C. (1991) *Accelerated Learning*. Hampshire, UK: Accelerated Learning Systems.

Rossi, E. (1991) *The 20 Minute Break*. New York: Tarcher Inc.

Rossi, E. (1994) *Psychobiology of Mind Body Healing*. New York: WW Norton.

Scheele, P. (1995) *The Photo-reading Whole Mind System*. London: Hodder and Stoughton.

Schwartz, D.J. (1986) *Maximise your Mental Power*. London: Thorsons.

Smith, M.J. (1975) *When I say No I Feel Guilty*. London: Bantum Press.

Szantesson, I. (1994) *Mind Mapping and Memory*. London: Kogan Page.

Tame, D. (1984) *The Secret Power of Music*. Northamptonshire, UK: Destiny Books.

Templar, R. (2001) *Fast Thinking Difficult People*. London: Financial Times Prentice Hall.

Templar, R. (2001) *Fast Thinking Work Overload*. London: Financial Times Prentice Hall.

Yates, F.A. (1994) *The Art of Memory*. London: Pimlico.

momentum prescription – Let Us Help You Work Out Which Book Will Suit Your Symptoms

Feel stuck in a rut? Something wrong and need help doing something about it?

◆ If you need tools to help making changes in your life: **coach yourself** (a good general guide to change)

◆ If you are considering dramatic career change: **snap, crackle or stop**

◆ If you need to work out what you'd like to be doing and how to get there: **be your own career consultant**

◆ If you need help making things happen and tackling the 'system' at work/in life: **change activist**

Feel that you can never make decisions and you just let things 'happen'?

◆ If you need help making choices: **the big difference**

◆ If you want to feel empowered and start making things happen for yourself: **change activist**

Feel life is too complicated and overwhelming?

◆ If you need help working through office politics and complexity: **clued up**

◆ If you need a kick up the backside to get out of your commerce-induced coma: **change activist**

◆ If you need an amusing and very helpful modern life survival guide: **innervation**

◆ If you never have enough time or energy to get things done or think properly: **mental space**

Feel like you might be in the wrong job?

◆ If you want help finding your destiny job and inspiration to make that dramatic career change: **snap, crackle or stop**

◆ If you feel like you aren't doing a job that is really 'what you are about': **soultrader**

◆ If you are struggling with the 'do something worthwhile OR make money dilemma': **change activist**

Feel that you're not the person/leader you should be?

◆ If you want to be the kind of person others want to follow: **lead yourself**

◆ If you need help becoming the person you've always wanted to be: **reinvent yourself**

◆ If you want to work out everything you've got to offer, and how to improve that: **grow your personal capital**

Feel you need help getting your ideas into action?

◆ If the problem is mainly other people, lack of time and the messiness of life: **clued up**

◆ If the problem is communicating your thinking: **hey you!**

◆ If the problem is more ideas than time and you are a bit overwhelmed with work: **mental space**

◆ If the problem is making change in your life: **coach yourself**

Feel you aren't projecting yourself and managing your career as well as you should?

◆ If you'd like to be the kind of person people think of first: **managing brand me**

◆ If you'd like people to listen to your ideas more readily: **hey you!**

◆ If you'd like to come across as the person you really are inside: **soultrader**

◆ If you need general help in changing the way you work/life: **coach yourself**

◆ If you need help working out what you've got and how best to use it: **float you**

Feel you'd like to be much more creative and a real 'ideas person'

◆ If you need inspiration on how to be innovative and think creatively: **innervation**

◆ If you need help spreading your ideas and engendering support: **hey you!**